DESKS
You Can Customize

BETTERWAY BOOKS

Read This Important Safety Notice

To prevent accidents, keep safety in mind while you work. Use the safety guards installed on power equipment; they are for your protection. When working on power equipment, keep fingers away from saw blades, wear safety goggles to prevent injuries from flying wood chips and sawdust, wear ear protection to protect your hearing, and consider installing a dust vacuum to reduce the amount of airborne sawdust in your woodshop. Don't wear loose clothing, such as neckties or shirts with loose sleeves, or jewelry, such as rings, necklaces or bracelets, when working on power equipment, and tie back long hair to prevent it from getting caught in your equipment. People who are sensitive to certain chemicals should check the chemical content of any product before using it. The author and editors who compiled this book have tried to make all the contents as accurate and correct as possible. Plans, illustrations, photographs and text have been carefully checked. All instructions, plans and projects should be carefully read, studied and understood before beginning construction. Due to the variability of local conditions, construction materials, skill levels, etc., neither the authors nor Betterway Books assumes any responsibility for any accidents, injuries, damages or other losses incurred resulting from the material presented in this book.

00   99   98   97   96   5   4   3   2   1

Library of Congress Cataloging-in-Publication Data

Graves, Garth.
    Desks you can customize / Garth Graves.
      p.   cm. — (Betterway woodworking plans series)
    Includes index.
    ISBN 1-55870-412-4 (pbk. : alk. paper)
    1. Desks. 2. Furniture making. I. Title. II. Series.
TT197.5.D4G73 1996
684.1′4—dc20
                             96-240
                             CIP

Editor: Adam Blake
Content Editor: Tom Begnal
Production Editor: Marilyn Daiker
Cover Designer: Sandy Kent
Cover Photographer: Garth Graves
Interior Designer: Brian Roeth
Illustrators: Garth Graves, Bob Shreve

A Word About Dimensions

The author and editors who compiled the information for this book have gone over all of the dimensions, drawings, photographs, text and captions to ensure that the information here is accurate. The best woodworkers plan projects through before they cut the first piece of wood. Please take the time to go over all of the dimensions for your project whether you are designing your own or building a project straight out of the book. This practice will not only ensure that you do not waste any wood, but will give you a unique understanding and appreciation of the furniture you are about to build.

METRIC CONVERSION CHART		
TO CONVERT	**TO**	**MULTIPLY BY**
Inches	Centimeters	2.54
Centimeters	Inches	0.4
Feet	Centimeters	30.5
Centimeters	Feet	0.03
Yards	Meters	0.9
Meters	Yards	1.1
Sq. Inches	Sq. Centimeters	6.45
Sq. Centimeters	Sq. Inches	0.16
Sq. Feet	Sq. Meters	0.09
Sq. Meters	Sq. Feet	10.8
Sq. Yards	Sq. Meters	0.8
Sq. Meters	Sq. Yards	1.2
Pounds	Kilograms	0.45
Kilograms	Pounds	2.2
Ounces	Grams	28.4
Grams	Ounces	0.04

ABOUT THE AUTHOR

Garth Graves has been a woodworker for thirty-five years, designing and producing projects for his home, boat and for woodworking publications. He is the author/illustrator of *Yacht Craftsman's Handbook* (International Marine Publishing/TAB Books/McGraw-Hill, 1992) and a contributor to *WoodenBoat, Classic Boat, Fine Woodworking, Popular Woodworking* and *Better Homes and Gardens* magazines.

To my wife of well over three decades (including the well over three months of this project)

Part One: Projects

Here are designs, dimensions and construction steps for you to build the writing desk, pedestal desk or secretary desk of your choice.

Learn how to make a writing desk that complements the design and style of your home. Choose one of the three styles shown here and adapt the parts as you see fit.

Solid Top

Frame-and-Panel Top

Lectern

In this chapter, you will see how to make a pedestal desk that is both attractive and practical. With information found in later chapters, you can make a desk that looks and functions like a traditional writing desk or a computer work station.

Craftsman-Style Single-Pedestal

With Turned Legs

Classic Style

Choose what style of secretary desk you want to make. Make it from solid wood or plywood, in one piece or two, or with the base open or enclosed.

Classic

Traditional

Country-Style

Part Two: Techniques

Building to suit your needs may involve an array of techniques applied to components of the project. Here are some of the techniques for the writing desk, pedestal desk or secretary desk of your choice.

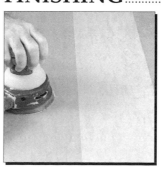

How This Book Works

Desks You Can Customize presents mix-and-match versions of three desk styles—writing desks, pedestal desks and secretary desks. Each style is constructed using a different method: solid planked, frame-and-panel, and veneer shell. Several variations of each style are presented, allowing you to blend personal taste, style and need into each project.

Obviously you won't combine cabriole legs with heavy craftsman-style legs or a Bauhaus cabinet, but there are many combinations that go well together. A number of them are pictured in this book. The objective is to offer a variety of writing desk options you can build to suit. There are three versions of each desk style. In part two of the book, variations are presented in a menu from which to mix and match.

Hopefully the designs presented will suit your taste and needs. Your style will be imprinted on the project by the design and materials you select and how you craft them. If the things you build tend to be scant, lighten up on the recommended stock. If your signature is toward heavier furniture, go heavier on the stock. The changes and modifications you make are going to depict your style.

PART ONE

PROJECTS

CHAPTER ONE

WRITING DESKS

Sometimes referred to as ladies' desks, these pieces are typically small and slight. Three designs are featured in this chapter: (1) a writing desk with tapered legs and a solid top (see photo at right); (2) a writing desk with cabriole legs and a frame-and-panel top (see figure 1-2); and (3) a lectern-style writing desk (see figure 1-3). Because all three desks have similar upper frame designs, you can interchange the tops, legs and organizers to create a variety of unique designs.

The organizers make an attractive and practical addition to any of the desks. The open-top version is shown in the photo, but the desk design lends itself to a hinged lift-lid enclosure as shown in the Lectern Desk project, or even a tamboured top. Such an organizer could be full width or offset to the left or right of the desk's center. Chapter eight details the procedure for making a basic organizer.

Normal desktop height is 27" to 29", but the desk can be made taller if you like (perhaps to fit a favorite chair). Lectern height is 40" to 44".

The desk you build can be as simple as a solid top, with or without a short vertical backstop. The desk in the photo has a solid top made from edge-glued boards, but a frame-and-panel top, with a leather or laminate panel, might better suit your style. A frame-and-panel top version of this desk is shown in figure 1-2 on page 10. The Pedestal Desk project in chapter two also has a frame-and-panel top.

This solid-top writing desk will add a touch of elegance to any room. The traditional desktop organizer is an attractive option that adds convenient storage space.

Variations suitable for this project include
1. Tapered legs
2. Straight legs
3. Turned legs (straight taper or beaded)
4. Cabriole legs
5. Cross-lapped leg frame (lectern)

Writing Desks

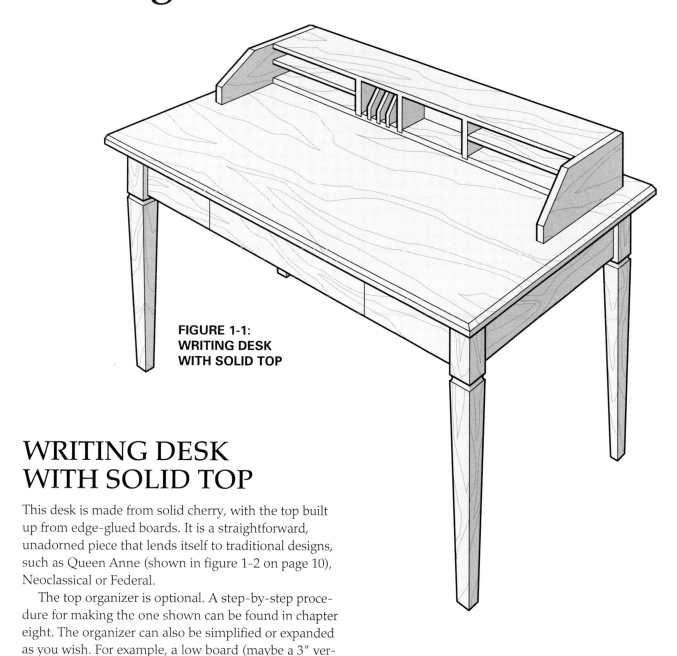

**FIGURE 1-1:
WRITING DESK
WITH SOLID TOP**

WRITING DESK
WITH SOLID TOP

This desk is made from solid cherry, with the top built up from edge-glued boards. It is a straightforward, unadorned piece that lends itself to traditional designs, such as Queen Anne (shown in figure 1-2 on page 10), Neoclassical or Federal.

The top organizer is optional. A step-by-step procedure for making the one shown can be found in chapter eight. The organizer can also be simplified or expanded as you wish. For example, a low board (maybe a 3" vertical backstop) let in along the back would be a good addition to this design.

WRITING DESK WITH A FRAME-AND-PANEL TOP

In this design, the solid top is replaced with a center panel inset surrounded by a frame. This gives the table an entirely different look. What you put in the center panel is your choice. Possibilities include leather (either real or simulated), veneer plywood of the same material, or any of the laminated composite countertops in matte black or a complementing color. Writing surfaces should be smooth, so stay away from embossed materials.

You could get the same but more subtle look by cutting a V-shaped or half-round groove inset from the solid top edge, thus framing the work surface.

Chapters two and three offer frame-and-panel details that might be applied. Chapter four discusses joinery options, including miters, splines, biscuits, dowels, cross-laps and mortise-and-tenon joints. A tongue cut along the edges of the plywood substrate (or veneer plywood if used) fits into grooves cut in the frame parts.

If you choose to build a frame-and-panel top, consider using cabriole or turned legs to give the entire desk a more traditional look. Cabriole and turned legs are discussed in chapter five.

With this added embellishment comes the opportunity to be more ornate with the legs and desk organizer. Consider adding the following:

Queen Anne legs—bought or shaped
Decorative organizer/shell
Traditional moulding around tabletop and shell

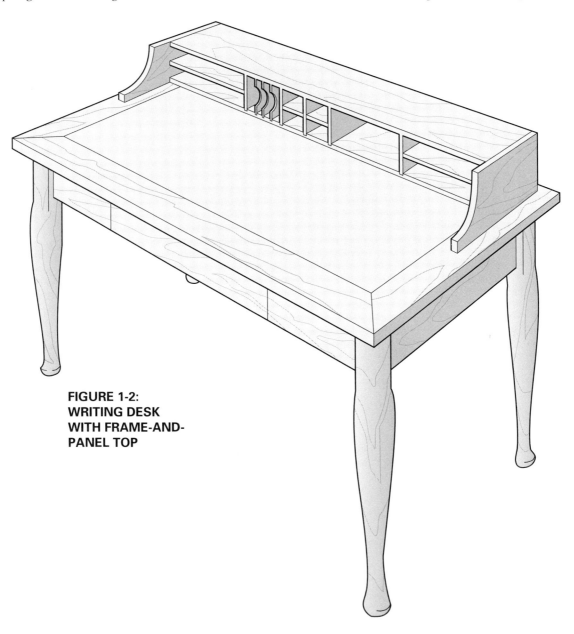

FIGURE 1-2: WRITING DESK WITH FRAME-AND-PANEL TOP

LECTERN DESK

Using either of the top designs previously described, this example includes a variation in height, a different leg style and a lift-lid enclosure.

For this taller desk, you might also consider making the top a bit smaller. As you add height, you also add mass, especially with the full-size organizer. You could reduce the desktop size by 25 percent or more for this variation. Think of Bob Cratchit hunched over his desk and the visual proportions that mental image portrays.

With added height comes added structural requirements for the taller leg stand. This version uses $\frac{3}{4}$" x $2\frac{1}{4}$"

and $\frac{3}{4}$" x 3" stock (joined at right angles) for the legs, but it could be built from heavier stock. Tapered, turned or square legs can also be made heavier if necessary. Also, with the added height, consider bracing the legs as shown.

The lift-lid organizer is optional, as is whether the primary work surface will be inside or on top of the shell. As shown in figure 1-6B on page 17, the lid face is attached to the lid for an inside work surface. However, if the work surface is on top, the lid face can be attached to the sides. Chapter eight suggests a few other organizer ideas. The organizer top is secured to the back and sides with countersunk screws. The screws are covered with wood plugs.

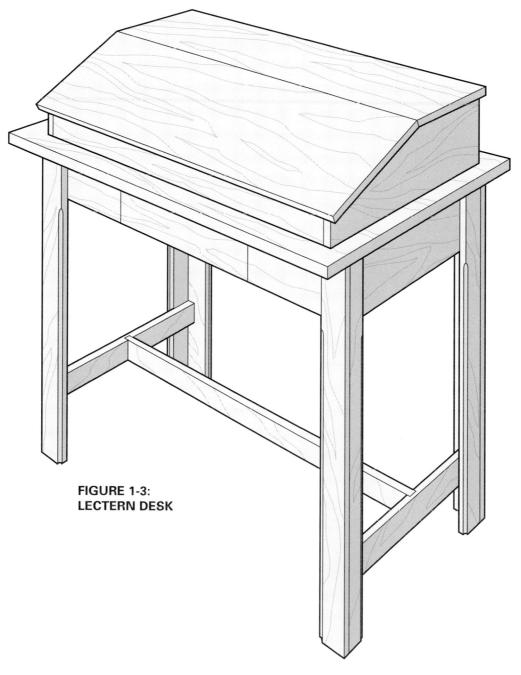

**FIGURE 1-3:
LECTERN DESK**

Writing Desk With Solid Top
DIMENSIONS

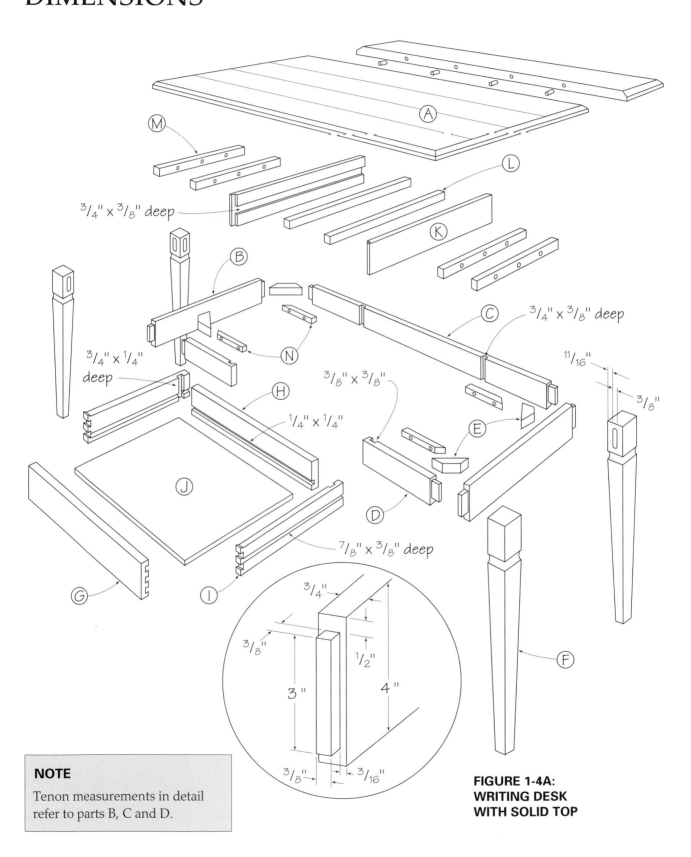

$^3/_4" \times ^3/_8"$ deep

$^3/_4" \times ^1/_4"$ deep

$^3/_8" \times ^3/_8"$

$^1/_4" \times ^1/_4"$

$^3/_4" \times ^3/_8"$ deep

$^{11}/_{16}"$

$^3/_8"$

$^7/_8" \times ^3/_8"$ deep

$^3/_4"$

$^3/_8"$

$^1/_2"$

$3"$

$4"$

$^3/_8"$

$^3/_{16}"$

**FIGURE 1-4A:
WRITING DESK
WITH SOLID TOP**

NOTE

Tenon measurements in detail
refer to parts B, C and D.

Organizer With Angled Ends

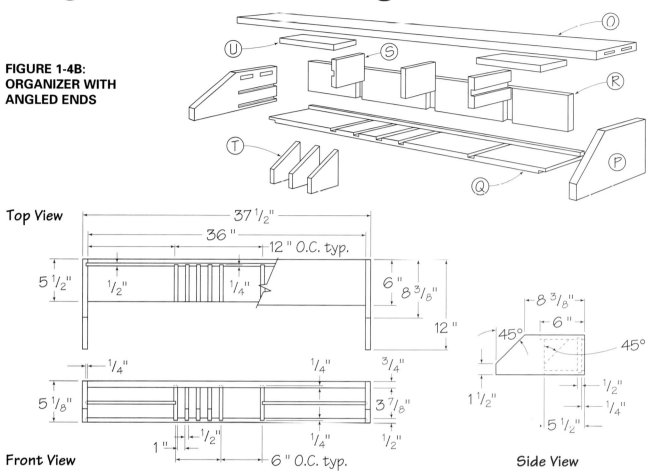

**FIGURE 1-4B:
ORGANIZER WITH
ANGLED ENDS**

Top View

37 1/2"

36 "

12 " O.C. typ.

5 1/2"   1/2"   1/4"   6 "   8 3/8"   12 "

1/4"   1/4"   3/4"

5 1/8"   3 7/8"

1 "   1/2"   1/4"   1/2"

6 " O.C. typ.

Front View

Side View

8 3/8"   6 "   45°

45°

1 1/2"   1/2"   1/4"   5 1/2"

CUTTING LIST—WRITING DESK WITH SOLID TOP

Desk

(A)	Top		³/₄" x 24" x 40³/₄"	Cherry
(B)	Side Apron	(2)	³/₄" x 4" x 18"*	Cherry
(C)	Rear Apron		³/₄" x 4" x 34³/₄"*	Cherry
(D)	Front Apron	(2)	³/₄" x 4" x 7³/₈"**	Cherry
(E)	Corner Brace	(4)	1¹/₄" x 1³/₄" x 4"	Cherry
(F)	Leg	(4)	1³/₄" x 1³/₄" x 27"	Cherry
(G)	Drawer Face		³/₄" x 4" x 20"	Cherry
(H)	Drawer Back		³/₄" x 4" x 19"	Alder
(I)	Drawer Side	(2)	³/₄" x 4" x 17¹/₂"	Alder
(J)	Drawer Bottom		¹/₈" x 19" x 16¹/₂"	Masonite
(K)	Drawer Guide	(2)	³/₄" x 4" x 19"***	Cherry
(L)	Drawer Runner	(2)	³/₄" x ³/₄" x 18"	Cherry
(M)	Long Cleat	(4)	³/₄" x ³/₄" x 12"	Cherry
(N)	Short Cleat	(4)	³/₄" x ³/₄" x 4"	Cherry

Organizer

(O)	Top		³/₄" x 6" x 36"	Cherry
(P)	Side	(2)	³/₄" x 5¹/₈" x 12"	Cherry
(Q)	Bottom		¹/₂" x 5¹/₂" x 36¹/₂"****	Cherry
(R)	Back		¹/₂" x 4³/₈" x 36¹/₂"	Cherry
(S)	Partition	(3)	¹/₂" x 5" x 4³/₈"	Cherry
(T)	Divider	(3)	¹/₂" x 5" x 4¹/₈"	Cherry
(U)	Shelf	(2)	¹/₂" x 4³/₄" x 12¹/₄"	Cherry

   * Includes ³/₈"-long tenons each end
  ** Includes ³/₈"-long tenon one end
 *** Includes ³/₈"-long rabbet one end
**** Includes ¹/₄"-long rabbets each end

NOTE
See chapter eight for details on
organizer construction.

Writing Desk With Frame-and-Panel Top
DIMENSIONS

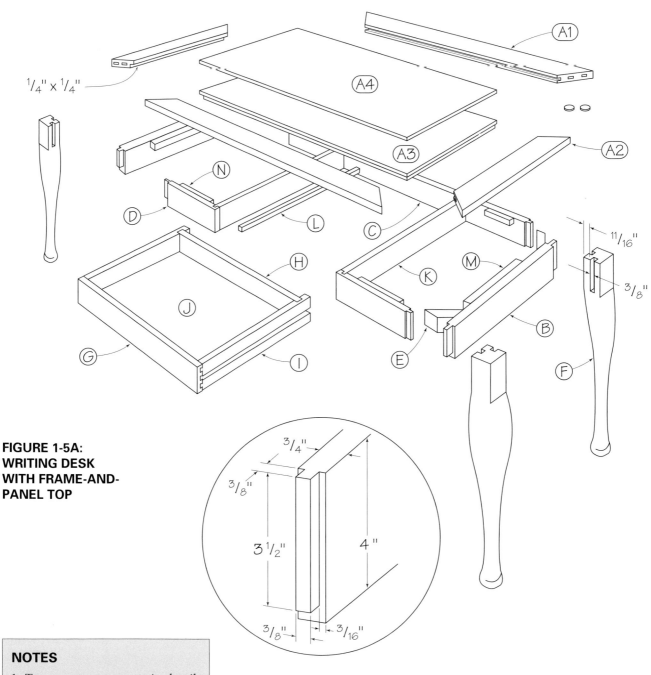

FIGURE 1-5A:
WRITING DESK
WITH FRAME-AND-
PANEL TOP

NOTES

1. Tenon measurements in detail refer to parts B, C and D.

2. Exploded views of the drawer and apron are shown on page 12, Writing Desk With Solid Top.

Organizer With Curved Ends

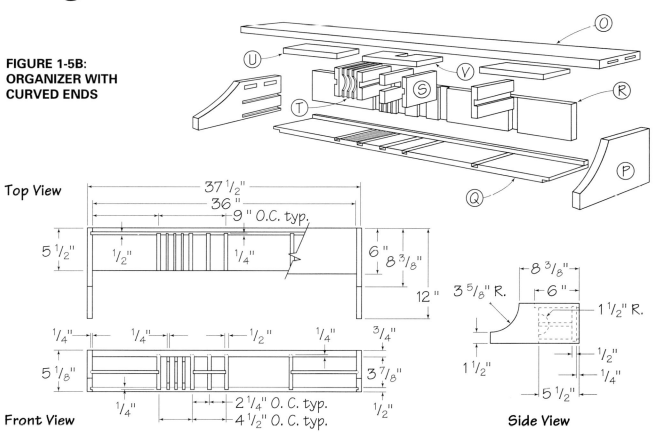

**FIGURE 1-5B:
ORGANIZER WITH
CURVED ENDS**

Top View

Front View

Side View

CUTTING LIST—WRITING DESK WITH FRAME-AND-PANEL TOP

Desk

(A1)	Top Side	(2) $^3/_4$" x 4" x 40$^3/_4$"	Cherry
(A2)	Top End	(2) $^3/_4$" x 4" x 24"	Cherry
(A3)	Top Substrate	$^5/_8$" x 16$^3/_8$" x 33$^1/_8$"	Plywood
(A4)	Top Laminate	$^1/_{16}$" x 16" x 32$^3/_4$"	Formica
(B)	Side Apron	(2) $^3/_4$" x 4" x 18"*	Cherry
(C)	Rear Apron	$^3/_4$" x 4" x 34$^3/_4$"*	Cherry
(D)	Front Apron	(2) $^3/_4$" x 4" x 7$^3/_8$"**	Cherry
(E)	Corner Brace	(4) 1$^1/_4$" x 1$^3/_4$" x 4"	Cherry
(F)	Cabriole Leg	(4) 1$^3/_4$" x 1$^3/_4$" x 27"	Cherry
(G)	Drawer Face	$^3/_4$" x 4" x 20"	Cherry
(H)	Drawer Back	$^3/_4$" x 4" x 19"	Alder
(I)	Drawer Side	(2) $^3/_4$" x 4" x 17$^1/_2$"	Alder
(J)	Drawer Bottom	$^1/_8$" x 19" x 16$^1/_2$"	Masonite
(K)	Drawer Guide	(2) $^3/_4$" x 4" x 19"***	Cherry
(L)	Drawer Runner	(2) $^3/_4$" x $^3/_4$" x 18"	Cherry
(M)	Long Cleat	(4) $^3/_4$" x $^3/_4$" x 12"	Cherry
(N)	Short Cleat	(4) $^3/_4$" x $^3/_4$" x 4"	Cherry

Organizer

(O)	Top	$^3/_4$" x 6" x 36"	Cherry
(P)	Side	(2) $^3/_4$" x 5$^1/_8$" x 12"	Cherry
(Q)	Bottom	$^1/_2$" x 5$^1/_2$" x 36$^1/_2$"****	Cherry
(R)	Back	$^1/_2$" x 4$^3/_8$" x 36$^1/_2$"	Cherry
(S)	Partition	(5) $^1/_2$" x 4$^3/_8$" x 5"	Cherry
(T)	Divider	(3) $^1/_4$" x 4$^3/_8$" x 5"	Cherry
(U)	Shelf	(2) $^1/_2$" x 4$^3/_4$" x 9$^1/_4$"	Cherry
(V)	Notched Shelf	$^1/_2$" x 4$^1/_2$" x 4$^3/_4$"	Cherry

* Includes $^3/_8$"-long tenons each end
** Includes $^3/_8$"-long tenon one end
*** Includes $^3/_8$"-long rabbet one end
**** Includes $^1/_4$"-long rabbets each end

NOTE
See chapter eight for details on
organizer construction.

Lectern Desk
DIMENSIONS

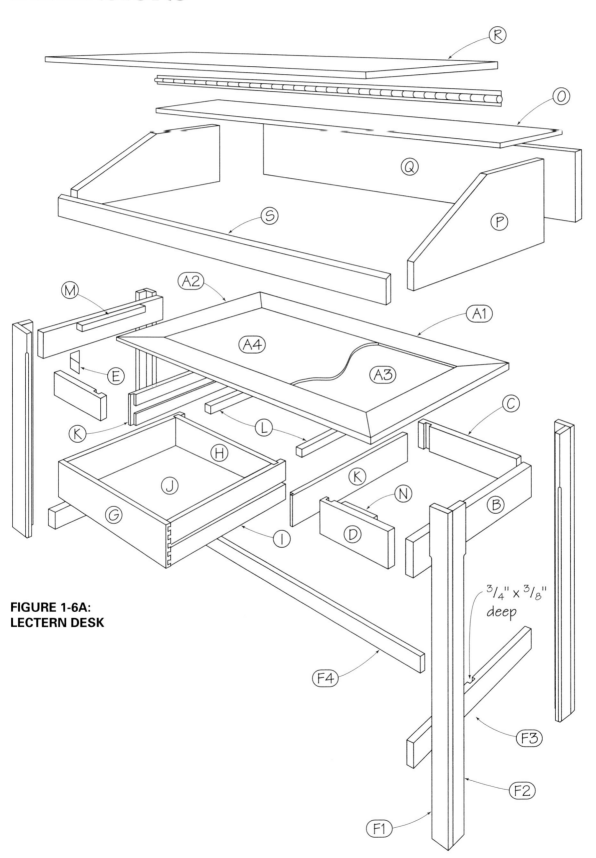

**FIGURE 1-6A:
LECTERN DESK**

$^3/_4$" x $^3/_8$"
deep

Organizer With Lift Lid

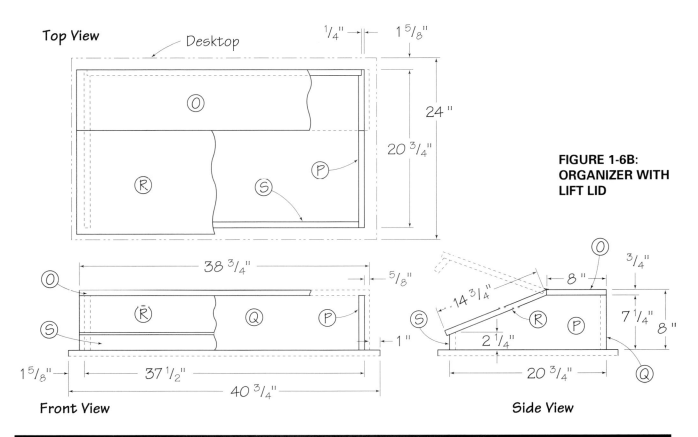

Top View

Desktop

¼"

1⁵⁄₈"

O

24 "

20³⁄₄"

P

R

S

**FIGURE 1-6B:
ORGANIZER WITH
LIFT LID**

38³⁄₄"

5⁄₈"

O

R

Q

P

S

1"

1⁵⁄₈"

37½"

40³⁄₄"

Front View

3⁄₄"

O

8 "

14³⁄₄"

7¼"

8 "

S

R

P

2¼"

Q

20³⁄₄"

Side View

CUTTING LIST—LECTERN DESK

Desk

(A1)	Top Side	(2)	¾" x 4" x 40¾"	Cherry
(A2)	Top End	(2)	¾" x 4" x 24"	Cherry
(A3)	Top Substrate		⁵⁄₈" x 16³⁄₈" x 33¹⁄₈"	Plywood
(A4)	Top Laminate		¹⁄₁₆" x 16" x 32¾"	Formica
(B)	Side Apron	(2)	¾" x 4" x 19¼"	Cherry
(C)	Rear Apron		¾" x 4" x 34½"	Cherry
(D)	Front Apron	(2)	¾" x 4" x 7¼"	Cherry
(E)	Corner Brace	(4)	1¼" x 1³⁄₄" x 4"	Cherry
(F1)	Leg Facing	(4)	¾" x 3" x 36"	Cherry
(F2)	Leg Side	(4)	¾" x 2¼" x 36"	Cherry
(F3)	Leg Side Brace	(2)	¾" x 2" x 19¼"	Cherry
(F4)	Leg Cross Brace		¾" x 2" x 35¼"	Cherry
(G)	Drawer Face		¾" x 4" x 20"	Cherry
(H)	Drawer Back		¾" x 4" x 19"	Alder
(I)	Drawer Side	(2)	¾" x 4" x 17½"	Alder

(J)	Drawer Bottom		¹⁄₈" x 19" x 16½"	Masonite
(K)	Drawer Guide	(2)	¾" x 4" x 18½"*	Cherry
(L)	Drawer Runner	(2)	¾" x ³⁄₄" x 17½"	Cherry
(M)	Long Cleat	(4)	¾" x ³⁄₄" x 12"	Cherry
(N)	Short Cleat	(4)	¾" x ³⁄₄" x 4"	Cherry

Organizer

(O)	Top		¾" x 8" x 38¾"	Cherry
(P)	Side	(2)	¾" x 7¼" x 20¾"	Cherry
(Q)	Back		½" x 7¼" x 37"	Cherry
(R)	Lid		¾" x 14¾" x 38¾"	Cherry
(S)	Lid Face		¾" x 2¼" x 35⁷⁄₈"	Cherry

* Includes ³⁄₈"-long rabbet one end

NOTE
See chapter eight for details on
organizer construction.

Writing Desks
MAKING THE SOLID TOP

Various methods are used to join the edges of the boards. They include the tongue and groove, splines, biscuits, milled glue-joint edges and old-fashioned dowel pins. Being old-fashioned, I doweled the joints.

The first order of business is to buy wood for the top. Nominal 1" lumber can vary in thickness but nets somewhere around ³⁄₄". Select stock that is flat, straight and true. Squareness is a must, whether you buy stock surfaced four sides (S4S) or plane the edges with a jointer or hollow-ground table saw blade.

The color, figuring and stability of wood are important factors to consider when building desktops or other such wide surfaces. Whether using cherry or other premium woods, select stock that fits your taste. Highly figured wood looks entirely different than straight-grained wood. Most purveyors of hardwoods offer such a choice. Check the ends of your stock for any checks or splits. Any that are found should be cut off well in front of the imperfection before starting.

Glue setup time varies with the family of glue you select. Woodworker's (yellow) glues are typically an aliphatic resin and are generally superior to white glue. Woodworker's glues are sandable, relatively clear and have good adhesion. Hide glue has good holding power but is dark in color. Two part epoxies are suitable for gluing dissimilar materials, but too much clamping pressure can squeeze the epoxy from between the joint. Either epoxy or contact cement works well when applying a facing or dissimilar materials, such as the tabletop panel.

CONSTRUCTION STEPS

STEP 1
Cut Stock to Size

Rip and crosscut stock as needed for the top. It's a good idea to cut the stock a little on the long side. Later, after the boards have been edge-glued, the top can be trimmed to final length.

STEP 1

STEP 2

Joint the Edges

A glue joint has maximum strength when the mating surfaces are smooth, so you'll need to plane the edges of the stock with a jointer. However, if a quality hollow-ground saw blade is used to rip the stock in step 1, the edges might not require further smoothing.

To minimize tear-out when using the jointer, feed the stock so that the jointer knives are cutting with the grain. If the grain direction isn't obvious, inspect the cut to see which direction any blown-out fibers are oriented. If you still can't tell, the feed direction doesn't much matter.

STEP 3

Lay Out Top and Mark Dowel Pin Locations

To help keep the top flat, lay out the boards so that the end-grain growth rings radiate in opposite directions. For example, if the first board has rings rainbowing up, the next should have rings rainbowing down. Repeat this alternating pattern for all the boards. However, if a board has a bad surface flaw, it's best to turn the board so that the flaw is located on the underside of the top, regardless of the growth ring direction.

Now, working from a common end, measure and mark locations of the four dowel pins. At a point 2" to 3" from each end, mark for $\frac{3}{8}$"-diameter dowel holes, then space the remaining holes about 12" apart. Matching holes can be measured, marked and drilled in adjacent boards.

Layout With Dowel Centering Pins (Optional)

As an alternative to measuring both boards separately, you can measure, mark and drill holes in one edge of one board only. Insert dowel centering pins into the drilled holes, and align the ends of the boards. Press the mating board against the pins to mark the opposing hole centers. Drill corresponding holes at the pin marks. Voilà! The pinholes are aligned horizontally along the board length and vertically along the board height.

STEP 4

STEP 5

Drill the Dowel Pin Holes (Horizontal Method)

One advantage of the Shopsmith (multipurpose woodworking machine) is its lateral drilling feature. The stock is fully supported on the horizontal saw table, which sets the edge perpendicular to the advancing drill bit. With the boards facedown, all holes are the same distance from the top surface.

Advancing the spindle/chuck, drill ³/₈"-diameter holes to a depth equal to slightly more than one-half the dowel pin length. For example, a 1¹/₂"-long dowel pin has a ¹³/₁₆"-deep hole.

STEP 5

TIP

Poor Man's Centering Pins: Drive a small brad at the marked locations, square to the edge. Cut off the heads, leaving ¹/₁₆" exposed. Place the next board, properly aligned and flush to the end of the first board, and press the two boards together. Remove the brads. The puncture points provide the dowel hole center points.

STEP 6

Drill the Dowel Pin Holes (Vertical Method)

The holes can be drilled on a drill press. The jig shown helps align the holes perpendicular to the edge and also centers them along the thickness.

STEP 6

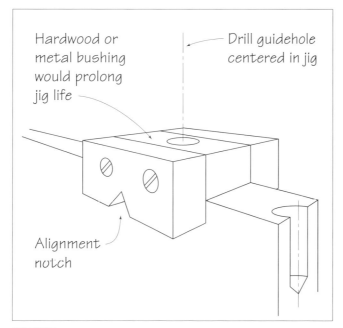

Hardwood or metal bushing would prolong jig life

Drill guidehole centered in jig

Alignment notch

STEP 7

Drill the Dowel Pin Holes (Portable Drill Method)

If you don't have a Shopsmith or a drill press, a portable drill with a guide can be used to drill the holes. The guide flanks the stock thickness to help keep the drill square to the edge.

STEP 7

Make the Dowel Pins

Use the band saw to cut $3/8$"-diameter dowel stock into $1^1/_2$" dowel pin lengths, then bevel the ends of the pins with a belt sander. The bevel makes it a little easier to insert the pins in the holes. To allow any excess glue to escape from the hole during assembly, cut a helical path along the pin using a scroll saw.

Somewhere along the way, I came across the jig shown. It makes cutting the grooves a lot easier. It is simply a solid block of wood (preferably hardwood) with a hole bored in the center. The hole diameter equals the diameter of the dowel stock. A screw, driven through one side of the block, projects into the hole. As the dowel stock is pushed through the hole, the tip of the screw cuts a straight groove in the dowel. If the dowel is rotated as it is pushed, a nice helix is cut. Once the grooves are cut, the dowel is crosscut into dowel pins.

You can also buy ready-made hardwood dowel pins at most hardware stores and building supply centers. They are available in a variety of diameters and lengths.

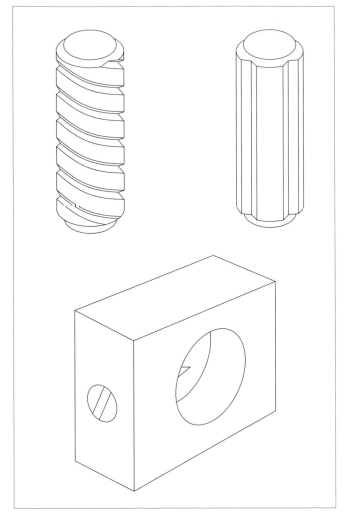

STEP 8

Assemble the First Two Boards

Don't attempt to bring all pieces together in a single squeeze, but rather work from one edge. Starting with the first two boards, add a thin coat of glue to the mating edges and to the holes and the dowel pins. Tap the pins into the holes, and assemble the two boards. With a little persuasion from a rubber mallet, begin driving the boards together, then bring them home with pipe clamps.

STEP 9

STEP 10

Assemble the Remaining Boards

Release the clamps, then add the next board in the same manner you joined the first two. Continue this procedure until all the boards have been assembled. You don't want the glue to start setting up, so work quickly throughout the glue-up process.

STEP 10

STEP 11

Clamp the Top

Three or four clamps are adequate for a top this size. Apply enough pressure to close the joints, but don't overtighten the clamps. Too much clamp pressure can cause much of the glue to squeeze out, resulting in a weakened joint. To keep the top from bowing as clamp pressure is applied, alternate the clamps, one on top, one on the bottom. Use a straightedge, as shown, to make sure the top is flat. If all looks OK, allow the glue to set overnight (or for as long as the manufacturer recommends).

STEP 11

Level the Surface

Using a chisel, carefully remove any glue beads that formed while clamping. Then check the surface of the top with a straightedge to see if it's level. Lay a straightedge across the top, and mark a line where the top meets the straightedge. Do this every 6″ along the surface. Where the lines start and stop will direct your sanding effort.

A sanding block should bring the top surface to finish quality. Leave your heavy-duty belt sander on the shelf; save it for something other than fine furniture. A high-speed palm sander or an orbital sander will bring the surface flat. It is kinder than a belt sander, but be aware that it can quickly produce an undulating surface unless a very light touch is used.

A tactile tool is also helpful. Slide your hand over the surface to detect slight rises and depressions you might not necessarily see. A halo light source (directed across the flat plane) can also help confirm flatness.

If the top is too far out of true, consider ripping and refitting the mismatched piece. Another choice is to have a lumber mill surface the top on a large thickness planer or thickness sander.

STEP 12

STEP 13

Trim the Top Square

The top is too big to trim on most table or radial arm saws. Using my Shopsmith, I clamp a guideblock (made from a length of straight scrap stock) under the top to ride alongside the saw table edge. The guide must be square to the edges of the top. The guideblock is held against the saw table edge as the trimming cut is made.

You can also use a portable circular saw to trim the top. Clamp a straightedge along the top surface, making sure it's square to the edges. Then, using the straightedge as a guide, make the trimming cut with the saw.

MAKING THE LEGS

The choice of leg styles may vary, but the attachment method remains the same for the two standard height writing desks. The lectern desk uses a different leg construction/attachment option. Various leg shapes are shown in chapter five, including details on how to cut the tapered legs.

Good strong joinery is paramount when building fine furniture. However, for this desk design, much of the rigidity comes from the desktop, so deep joints are not necessary. What is critical is solid joinery of the leg frame and solid attachment of the leg frame to the top.

Decide on the height and style of the four legs, then rip them into square blanks. If the blanks are to be turned, leave a common square block of 2x2 stock 5" down from the upper end (plus about 1" of working stock on both ends).

CONSTRUCTION STEPS

STEP 1
Choose the Joinery

Mortise-and-tenon joinery substantially increases the gluing area and provides lasting joints connecting legs and aprons. Some of the various kinds of mortise-and-tenon joints are shown. I used the blind mortise and tenon for the tapered leg construction detailed in the following steps, but the open mortise is also a good option here.

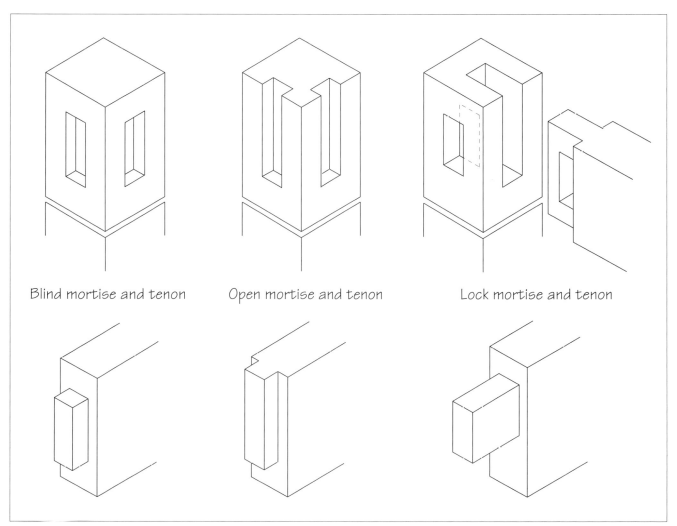

Blind mortise and tenon   Open mortise and tenon   Lock mortise and tenon

STEP 1

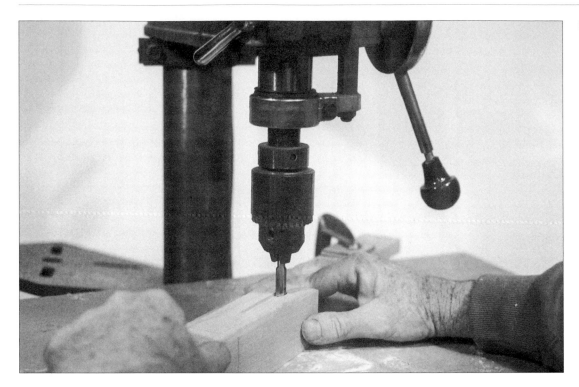

STEP 2

Cut the Mortises

It's easiest to cut the mortises while the legs are square. There are a number of ways to cut a blind mortise.

A straight router bit will do the job nicely. This can be driven with a drill press, as shown in the photo, or with your router, as described later. Set your drill press to the highest speed (big to little pulley 5" to 2" diameter rotates at around 5000 revolutions per minute [rpm]). The speed is slower than that of a portable router, but it's fast enough for this task.

If you lie awake wondering how fast your drill press rotates, you can calculate it by multiplying the diameter of the driving pulley times the motor rpm, then dividing the product by the diameter of the driven pulley. The calculation looks like this:

$$5 \text{ in.} \times 1800 \text{ rpm} = 9000 \text{ in. rpm}$$

$$\frac{9000 \text{ in. rpm}}{2 \text{ in.}} = 4500 \text{ rpm}$$

If your drill press doesn't have a tapered shaft (thereby locking the Jacob's chuck firmly to take the side loads), consider buying a socket spindle for your drill press if you plan to do more routing.

Set the stop on the quill to the mortise depth (³⁄₈" for this project). Clamp an auxiliary fence to the drill press table, centering the leg blank below the router bit along the tenon line. Mark the start and end positions on the worktable, or clamp a stopblock at the end of the run. In a series of shallow but progressively deeper cuts with each pass (cutting depth is a factor of wood hardness, bit sharpness, rpm and feed speed), run the stock along the auxiliary fence for the length of the mortise. Always advance the stock into cutter rotating toward the fence or guide.

Complete all eight cuts at the first depth, then lower the quill and repeat the procedure until you reach the final mortise depth. With all eight inside corner faces mortised, sand back any wood fibers that may have blown out as a result of the cut.

You can also cut the mortise using the portable drill or the drill press. Mark off the center line of the mortise positioned to receive the shouldered tenon. Remember to account for the radius of the drill bit when marking holes at the ends of the mortise. Using an awl, or other pointed object, poke hole center points along the mortise, spacing them at increments slightly less than the bit diameter. Drill holes to the proper depth. Clean out the remaining material with a sharp wood chisel. Use of a mortising bit to cut square corners while drilling out the stock will eliminate the chiseling requirement.

Square the ends of the mortise cut with a chisel, or leave them rounded. If left rounded, plan to round the top and bottom of the tenons to match the mortise.

STEP 3

Rout the Veining Detail

A router with a coving bit is used to make the veining detail. Clamp the four legs together, making sure the ends are flush. Clamp a straightedge across the legs to guide the router base. Set the coving bit to make a shallow cut, then pass the router over the legs. Be sure to keep the router base in contact with the straightedge while making the cut. Next, rotate each of the legs 90°, then reclamp the guide and again make the cut. Repeat this until all four sides are veined.

STEP 4

Shape the Legs

Refer to chapter five for a detailed procedure that explains how to cut square tapers. Other leg styles are also shown.

CUTTING THE APRONS, DRAWER GUIDES AND DRAWER

The side, rear and front aprons and the drawer guides are ripped to 4" widths. After ripping all the parts, they are cut to length. When cutting to length, be sure to allow for the 3/8"-long tenons on each end of the side and rear aprons and one end of the front apron.

There are a number of ways to cut tenons. The dado-head and table saw methods are discussed here. In chapter six, tenons are cut using the band saw. A well-cut tenon should "press fit" (not too tight or too sloppy) into the matching mortise.

CUTTING THE TENONS

CONSTRUCTION STEPS (DADO-HEAD METHOD)

STEP 1

Cut the Tenon Shoulders

Establish the tenon shoulder on the table saw. A fine-tooth, hollow-ground blade produces a smooth cut.

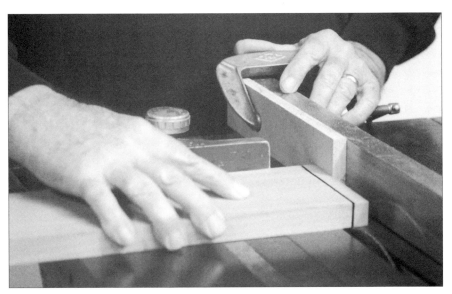

STEP 1

STEP 2

Clean Out the Remaining Stock

Use the table saw with a dado blade to complete the tenon.

STEP 2

STEP 3

Round the Ends

Using a chisel, round the tenon ends to match the radius cut in the mortise.

STEP 1

CUTTING THE TENONS

CONSTRUCTION STEPS (TABLE SAW METHOD)

Cut the Tenon Shoulders

This procedure is the same as step 1 above left.

Cut the Tenon Width

Set the blade to a height that equals the tenon length. Locate the rip fence so that the blade makes a cut establishing the tenon shoulder. With the stock held on end, pass the stock through the blade to make the first cut. Next, place the opposite face of the stock against the fence and repeat the cut.

STEP 2

Cut the Tenon Length

Tenons can be cut by hand or on the tablesaw using a tenoning jig as shown in the photo.

STEP 3

CUTTING THE DADOES AND GROOVES

The dado-head cutter will come in handy here. However, if you don't have a dado head, there are a couple of other options.

When equipped with a straight bit, the router does an excellent job cutting dadoes and grooves. Clamp a straightedge to the stock to guide the router during the cut. To minimize burning, limit the depth of cut to $\frac{1}{4}$" for each pass.

You can also cut dadoes and grooves by making multiple passes with a regular saw blade. It takes a little longer, but the job gets done just as well.

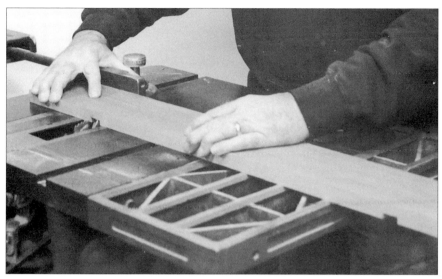

STEP 1

STEP 2

CONSTRUCTION STEPS

STEP 1

Dado the Rear Apron

Lay out and mark the location of the two dadoes in the rear apron. Use the table saw, equipped with a dado head, to make the cuts. Also lay out and cut the dado on the end of each front apron.

STEP 2

Make the Drawer Guides

Use the dado head to rabbet the front end of each drawer guide. Also using the dado head, cut the groove along the inside face of each piece as shown. The groove is centered on the 4"-wide stock.

Dry Assemble the Parts

To make sure everything fits well, it's a good idea to dry assemble all the parts. If a joint is especially tight, use a chisel to shave material as needed to get a smooth-sliding fit. A joint that's tight at dry assembly will be even more difficult to assemble once glue is added because the glue tends to swell the wood slightly.

STEP 3

Make the Drawers

Cut the drawer parts to size, then cut the groove for the bottom in the face, back and sides. See chapter seven for more information on making drawers. When installed, the top edge of the drawer face should be about $1/8$" below the underside of the desktop. Allow for this space when you mark the groove location on the drawer sides. Note that the groove starts at the back of the drawer side and is stopped at the base of the dovetails. This allows the drawer face to contact the front end of the runner, stopping the drawer flush with the front aprons.

STEP 4

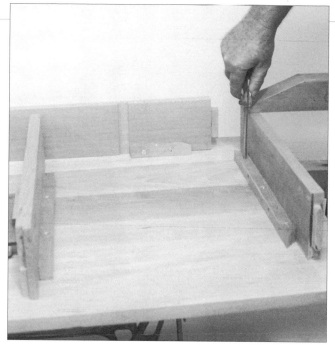

STEP 1

FINAL ASSEMBLY

Give all the parts a thorough sanding before starting the assembly. Soften any sharp edges or corners.

Everything that is needed for the assembly process should be at hand before you start. That includes such items as glue, clamps, screws and a screwdriver. Use clamp pads to protect the legs during clamping.

CONSTRUCTION STEPS

STEP 1

Assemble the Side Aprons

Cut stock for the long and short cleats to ¾" square, then cut the cleats to length. Bevel the ends as needed. Glue and screw the cleats to the aprons and drawer guides as shown in the exploded view on page 12. Attach the side aprons to the underside of the top with screws driven through the cleats. *The pilot holes through the cleats should be slightly oversized to allow the top to expand and contract with seasonal changes in moisture content.*

STEP 2

Assemble the Back Legs and Rear Apron

Glue the two back legs to the rear apron. Then glue the back legs/rear apron subassembly to the side aprons. Secure the rear apron cleats to the top as described in step 1.

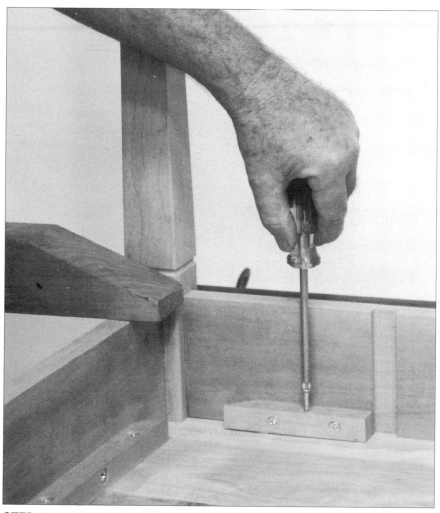

STEP 2

STEP 3

Add the Front Legs and Aprons

Glue the two front legs to the side aprons. Also glue the two front aprons to the front legs. Secure the front apron cleats to the top.

STEP 4

Add the Drawer Guides

Slip the drawer guides into the dadoes cut in the front and rear aprons. Check the parts for squareness, and fasten the cleats to the top.

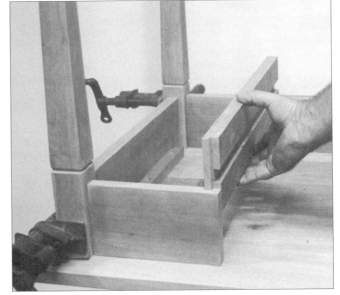

STEP 5

Brace the Corners, and Add the Drawer

Glue and screw corner braces for added rigidity. Add the drawer and check it for a smooth-sliding fit. If the drawer tends to bind, undercut the runners or widen the drawer-side groove as needed.

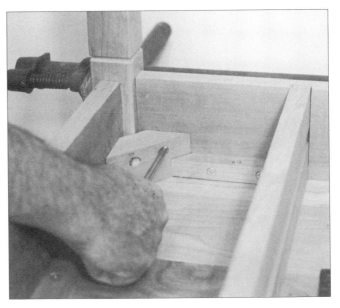

CHAPTER TWO

PEDESTAL DESKS

*This oak desk, influenced by the craftsman style, is a perfect size for a small room.
It can be easily expanded to a larger size by adding a second pedestal.*

Many of today's scribes, calligraphers and illustrators have traded in their pens and brushes for a mouse, keyboard, monitor and computer processing unit (CPU). Each desk in this chapter can be built to look and function like a traditional writing desk or tailored to serve as a computer work station. Three pedestal desk designs are offered here: (1) a craftsman-style desk that can be made with either a single or double pedestal (see photo above); (2) a

pedestal desk with turned legs (see figure 2-2); and (3) a classic-style pedestal desk (see figure 2-3).

Pedestal desks provide a variety of options for computer users. In the double-pedestal versions, the CPU (either a tower or horizontal chassis mounted on its side) can be enclosed behind a door or false drawer face in one of the pedestals. If you can get along without drawers, you can house the CPU in the single-pedestal desk.

You can also consider mounting the CPU on a slide-out base for access to connector ports, or cut an opening (with or without a door) in the back or inside the kneehole panel. Provide a raceway of some sort to route cables over the back edge or through the top to interconnect components. Mount a surge protector/quad outlet box at the back of the kneehole or inside a pedestal to power the system with one external power cord.

Pedestal Desks

FIGURE 2-1:
CRAFTSMAN-STYLE
SINGLE-PEDESTAL
DESK

CRAFTSMAN-STYLE SINGLE-PEDESTAL DESK

I built this desk to be used in a small studio apartment. Through the generosity of a sister-in-law, an older computer will soon be turning out newspaper articles at the hands of my journalist son. This desk project, made from oak, has a single pedestal on one end and a supporting end brace on the other. A sliding tray supports a computer keyboard. In the future, a printer rack will go on top. Another possible location for a printer would be in an open pedestal with a printer shelf. As shown in the inset, the addition of a second pedestal creates a larger and more impressive desk.

The desk's future home has a mixed bag of furniture styles, including a light oak canvas sling chair, a dresser from an unfinished furniture store and an oak drafting table. Oak was the wood of choice for the project, and my son's appreciation of the craftsman style influenced the design. Available floor space also was a consideration.

Lap joints are used here instead of the more traditional mortise-and-

tenon joints. The craftsman look, coupled with a little Greene and Greene architecture, resulted in the prominent joinery.

The end brace, which replaces the second pedestal, can be open (as shown in the photo on page 35) or paneled. For a computer desk, you could also play with the idea of lengthening the top to add an open-frame shelf below for a printer or plotter.

PEDESTAL DESK WITH TURNED LEGS

This desk has a more traditional style, with a mitered top frame. Consider using ½"-thick veneer plywood for the insert, let in around the top frame. Each pedestal side has four panels. The rails have mitered ends and are secured to notches cut in the legs.

A profile is turned on the bottom portion of the 27¼"-long legs. However, as an option, you can make short turning segments and peg them to the end of square legs. Commercially made turnings could be used here if you lack the time, tools or interest to produce your own. See chapter five for some additional leg variations.

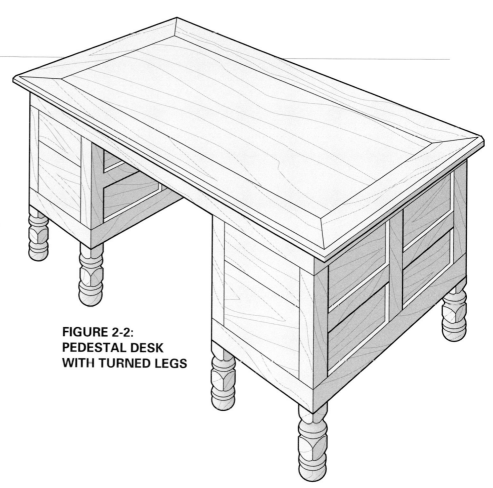

**FIGURE 2-2:
PEDESTAL DESK
WITH TURNED LEGS**

**FIGURE 2-3:
CLASSIC-STYLE
PEDESTAL DESK**

CLASSIC-STYLE PEDESTAL DESK

This floor-based, raised-panel desk offers a classical look for a grand library or study. A center drawer plus six pedestal drawers provide plenty of storage space.

The top frame is mitered. The center panel writing surface is a Formica-laminated plywood substrate. An inset leather or slate laminate could be substituted for the center panel.

A baseboard around the bottom of each pedestal is optional, but it is a nice detail that can add visual balance to the design. For further refinement, consider cutting a cove or other moulded detail along the top edge of the baseboard.

Craftsman-Style Pedestal Desk
DIMENSIONS

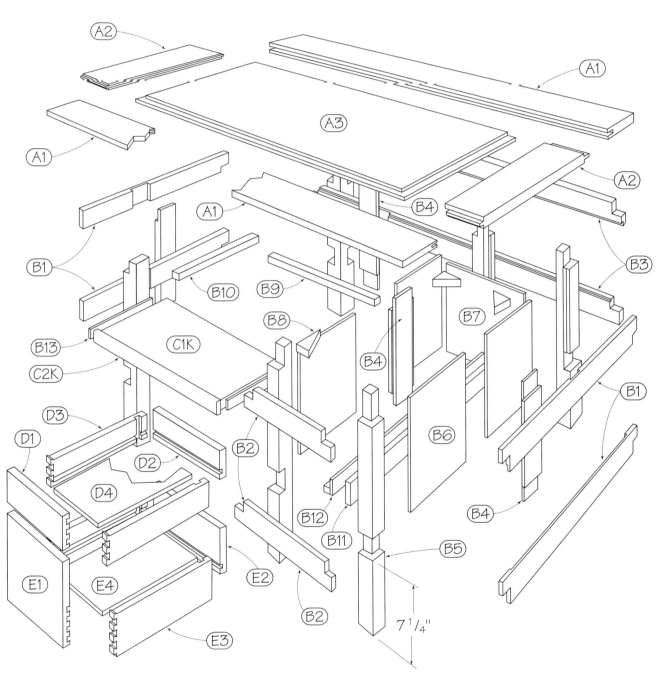

**FIGURE 2-4A:
CRAFTSMAN-STYLE
PEDESTAL DESK**

CUTTING LIST—CRAFTSMAN-STYLE SINGLE-PEDESTAL DESK

Top

(A1)	Side	(2)	$\frac{3}{4}$" x $3\frac{3}{4}$" x 40"	Oak
(A2)	End	(2)	$\frac{3}{4}$" x $3\frac{3}{4}$" x 17"*	Oak
(A3)	Inset		$\frac{1}{2}$" x 17" x 33"**	Oak Ply

Base

(B1)	Side Rail	(6)	$\frac{3}{4}$" x $2\frac{1}{2}$" x 22"***	Oak
(B2)	Front Rail	(2)	$\frac{3}{4}$" x $2\frac{1}{2}$" x $15\frac{1}{4}$"	Oak
(B3)	Back Rail	(2)	$\frac{3}{4}$" x $2\frac{1}{2}$" x 38"	Oak
(B4)	Stile	(4)	$\frac{3}{4}$" x $2\frac{1}{2}$" x 20"	Oak
(B5)	Leg	(6)	$1\frac{3}{4}$" x $1\frac{3}{4}$" x $27\frac{1}{4}$"****	Oak
(B6)	Side Panel	(4)	$\frac{3}{8}$" x $8\frac{3}{8}$" x $15\frac{3}{4}$"	Oak Ply
(B7)	Back Panel		$\frac{3}{8}$" x $12\frac{3}{8}$" x $15\frac{3}{4}$"	Oak Ply
(B8)	Corner Brace	(4)	$\frac{3}{4}$" x $4\frac{1}{4}$" x 6"	Oak
(B9)	Long Cleat		$\frac{3}{4}$" x $\frac{3}{4}$" x 21"	Oak
(B10)	Short Cleat	(3)	$\frac{3}{4}$" x $\frac{3}{4}$" x 10"	Oak
(B11)	Slide Cleat	(4)	1" x $2\frac{1}{2}$" x $18\frac{1}{2}$"	Oak
(B12)	Drawer Slide	(2 pairs)	$\frac{7}{8}$" x $1\frac{3}{4}$" x $18\frac{1}{2}$"	Accuride
(B13)	Keyboard Slide	(1 pair)	$\frac{17}{32}$" x $1\frac{1}{4}$" x 21"	Accuride

Keyboard Tray

(C1K)	Tray	$\frac{1}{2}$" x 14" x 19"	Oak Ply
(C2K)	Facing	$\frac{3}{4}$" x $1\frac{1}{4}$" x 21"	Oak

Upper Drawer

(D1)	Face		$\frac{3}{4}$" x $5\frac{1}{2}$" x $11\frac{3}{4}$"	Oak
(D2)	Back		$\frac{1}{2}$" x $5\frac{1}{2}$" x $11\frac{1}{4}$"	Oak
(D3)	Side	(2)	$\frac{1}{2}$" x $5\frac{1}{2}$" x $16\frac{3}{4}$"	Oak
(D4)	Bottom		$\frac{1}{8}$" x $11\frac{1}{4}$" x 16"	Masonite

Lower Drawer

(E1)	Face		$\frac{3}{4}$" x $9\frac{1}{2}$" x $11\frac{3}{4}$"	Oak
(E2)	Back		$\frac{1}{2}$" x 7" x $11\frac{1}{4}$"	Oak
(E3)	Side	(2)	$\frac{1}{2}$" x 7" x $16\frac{3}{4}$"	Oak
(E4)	Bottom		$\frac{1}{8}$" x $11\frac{1}{4}$" x 16"	Masonite

     * Includes $\frac{1}{4}$"-long tenons each end
    ** Includes $\frac{1}{4}$" rabbet all around
  *** On end brace, front end of rails not notched
 **** On end brace, front leg is notched on only one side

NOTES

1. If making double-pedestal desk, increase lengths of A1, A3 and B3.

2. Drawer construction shown here requires a fully concealed slide available from The Woodworker's Store (see Sources of Supply on page 126). Slide requires $\frac{1}{2}$"-thick drawer sides. Drawer bottom must be $\frac{1}{2}$" from bottom edge of drawer. Have slides on hand before building drawers. See chapter seven for details on drawer construction.

3. Keyboard slide available from The Woodworker's Store (see Sources of Supply on page 126).

4. Panels are cut $\frac{1}{8}$" narrow to allow for wood movement.

Pedestal Desk With Turned Legs
DIMENSIONS

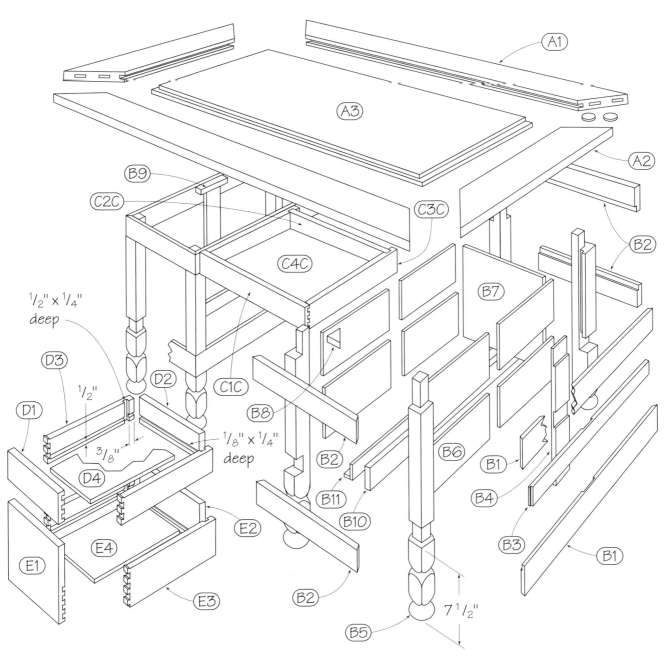

FIGURE 2-5A:
PEDESTAL DESK
WITH TURNED LEGS

CUTTING LIST—DOUBLE-PEDESTAL DESK WITH TURNED LEGS

Top

(A1)	Side	(2)	³/₄" x 4" x 53¹/₂"	Oak
(A2)	End	(2)	³/₄" x 4" x 30"	Oak
(A3)	Inset		¹/₂" x 22¹/₂" x 46"*	Oak Ply

Base

(B1)	Side Rail	(8)	³/₄" x 2¹/₂" x 28"	Oak
(B2)	Front/Back Rail	(8)	³/₄" x 2¹/₂" x 15¹/₄"	Oak
(B3)	Center Rail	(4)	³/₄" x 2¹/₂" x 25¹/₄"**	Oak
(B4)	Stile	(4)	³/₄" x 2¹/₂" x 20"	Oak
(B5)	Leg	(8)	1³/₄" x 1³/₄" x 27¹/₄"	Oak
(B6)	Side Panel	(16)	³/₈" x 11⁵/₈" x 7"	Oak Ply
(B7)	Back Panel	(2)	³/₈" x 12³/₈" x 15³/₄"	Oak Ply
(B8)	Corner Brace	(8)	³/₄" x 4" x 6"	Oak
(B9)	Cleat	(4)	³/₄" x ³/₄" x 6"	Oak
(B10)	Slide Cleat	(10)	as needed	Oak
(B11)	Drawer Slide	(5 pairs)	⁷/₈" x 1³/₄" x 18¹/₂"	Accuride

Center Drawer

(C1C)	Face		³/₄" x 2³/₈" x 21"	Oak
(C2C)	Back		¹/₂" x 2³/₈" x 20¹/₂"	Oak
(C3C)	Side	(2)	¹/₂" x 2³/₈" x 16³/₄"	Oak
(C4C)	Bottom		¹/₈" x 16" x 20¹/₂"	Masonite

Upper Drawer

(D1)	Face	(2)	³/₄" x 5¹/₂" x 11³/₄"	Oak
(D2)	Back	(2)	¹/₂" x 5¹/₂" x 11¹/₄"	Oak
(D3)	Side	(4)	¹/₂" x 5¹/₂" x 16³/₄"	Oak
(D4)	Bottom	(2)	¹/₈" x 11¹/₄" x 16"	Masonite

Lower Drawer

(E1)	Face	(2)	³/₄" x 9¹/₂" x 11³/₄"	Oak
(E2)	Back	(2)	¹/₂" x 7" x 11¹/₄"	Oak
(E3)	Side	(4)	¹/₂" x 7" x 16³/₄"	Oak
(E4)	Bottom	(2)	¹/₈" x 11¹/₄" x 16"	Masonite

* Includes ¹/₄" rabbet all around
** Includes ³/₈"-long rabbets each end

NOTES

1. Drawer construction shown here requires a fully concealed slide available from The Woodworker's Store (see Sources of Supply on page 126). Slide requires ¹/₂"-thick drawer sides. Drawer bottom must be ¹/₂" from bottom edge of drawer. Have slides on hand before building drawers. See chapter seven for details on drawer construction.

2. Panels are cut ¹/₈" narrow to allow for wood movement.

3. See figure 5-9B on page 94 for details on the turned legs used on this desk.

Classic-Style Pedestal Desk
DIMENSIONS

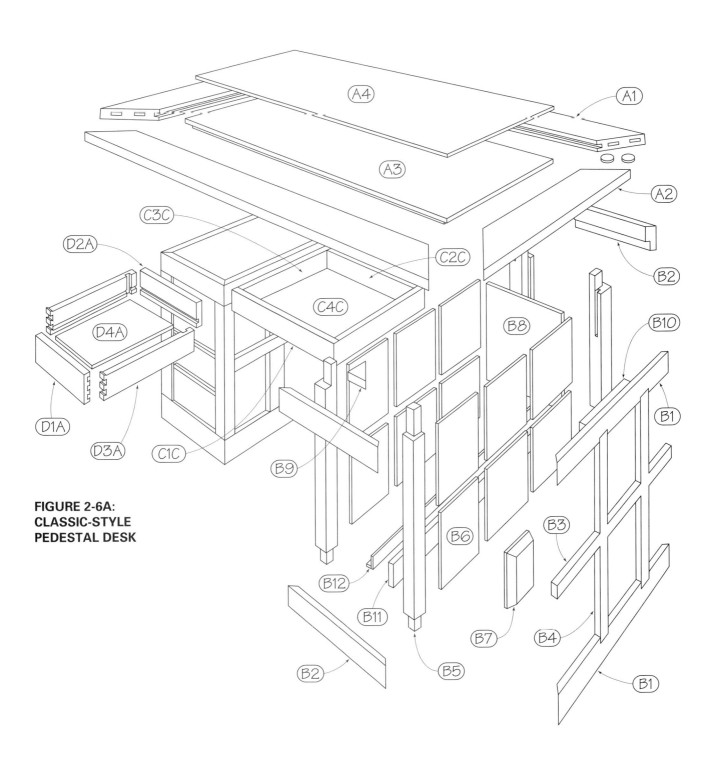

FIGURE 2-6A:
CLASSIC-STYLE
PEDESTAL DESK

CUTTING LIST—CLASSIC-STYLE PEDESTAL DESK

Top

(A1) Side	(2)	$^3/_4$" x 4" x $53^1/_2$"	Oak
(A2) End	(2)	$^3/_4$" x 4" x 30"*	Oak
(A3) Substrate		$^5/_8$" x $22^1/_2$" x 46"*	Plywood
(A4) Laminate		$^1/_{16}$" x 22" x $45^1/_2$"	Formica

Base

(B1) Side Rail	(8)	$^3/_4$" x $2^1/_2$" x 28"	Oak
(B2) Front/Back Rail	(8)	$^3/_4$" x $2^1/_2$" x $15^1/_4$"	Oak
(B3) Panel Rail	(4)	$^3/_4$" x $2^1/_2$" x $25^1/_4$"**	Oak
(B4) Panel Stile	(8)	$^3/_4$" x $2^1/_2$" x $27^1/_4$"	Oak
(B5) Leg	(8)	$1^3/_4$" x $1^3/_4$" x $27^1/_4$"	Oak
(B6) Side Panel	(24)	$^3/_8$" x $7^1/_8$" x $10^5/_8$"	Oak Ply
(B7) Applied Panel	(24)	$^1/_2$" x 5" x $8^5/_8$"	Oak
(B8) Back Panel	(2)	$^3/_8$" x $12^3/_8$" x 23"	Oak Ply
(B9) Corner Brace	(8)	$^3/_4$" x 4" x 6"	Oak
(B10) Cleat	(4)	$^3/_4$" x $^3/_4$" x 6"	Oak
(B11) Slide Cleat	(14)	as needed	Oak
(B12) Drawer Slide	(7 pairs)	$^7/_8$" x $1^3/_4$" x $18^1/_2$"	Accuride

Center Drawer

(C1C) Face		$^3/_4$" x $2^3/_8$" x 21"	Oak
(C2C) Back		$^1/_2$" x $2^3/_8$" x $20^1/_2$"	Oak
(C3C) Side	(2)	$^1/_2$" x $2^3/_8$" x $16^3/_4$"	Oak
(C4C) Bottom		$^1/_8$" x 16" x $20^1/_2$"	Masonite

Pedestal Drawer

(D1A) Face	(6)	$^3/_4$" x $7^3/_8$" x $11^3/_4$"	Oak
(D2A) Back	(6)	$^1/_2$" x $7^3/_8$" x $11^1/_4$"	Oak
(D3A) Side	(12)	$^1/_2$" x $7^3/_8$" x $16^3/_4$"	Oak
(D4A) Bottom	(6)	$^1/_8$" x $11^1/_4$" x 16"	Masonite

* Includes $^1/_4$" rabbet all around
** Includes $^3/_8$"-long rabbets each end

NOTES

1. Drawer construction shown here requires a fully concealed slide available from The Woodworker's Store (see Sources of Supply on page 126). Slide requires $^1/_2$"-thick drawer sides. Drawer bottom must be $^1/_2$" from bottom edge of drawer. Have slides on hand before building drawers. See chapter seven for details on drawer construction.

2. Panels are cut $^1/_8$" narrow to allow for wood movement.

Pedestal Desks
CONSTRUCTION NOTES

For the craftsman-style single-pedestal desk, the two back rails extend the length of the desk, connecting the end brace to the single pedestal. The double-pedestal designs have freestanding pedestals connected by the top, so the back rails are cut to only the pedestal width. Of course, you could use back rails cut to the full length of the desk here but not if you intend to "knock down" the desk to make it easier to move.

The distance between bases (the width of the kneehole and its center drawer) should be about 19" to 20". If the space is to be used for a pull-out keyboard, more than 20" may be better. Check the width of your keyboard before cutting any stock.

The legs are made from 1³/₄" square stock. The panels on the craftsman-style desk are unadorned. The turned leg desk has the same type of panel but more of them. The classic desk has an English look, with smaller raised panels. The style, size and proportion of the desk you build will dictate the best matrix to use for your project.

If your desk is to be used with a computer, figure 2-7 presents some component housings that can be applied to any of the projects in this chapter. Before starting, think about cable routes and the location of the CPU, printer and power source.

If you have a legal mind (and keep legal-size records), you'll want an inside drawer width of 14¹/₂". Letter-size files require an inside drawer width of 11¹/₂". The pedestal

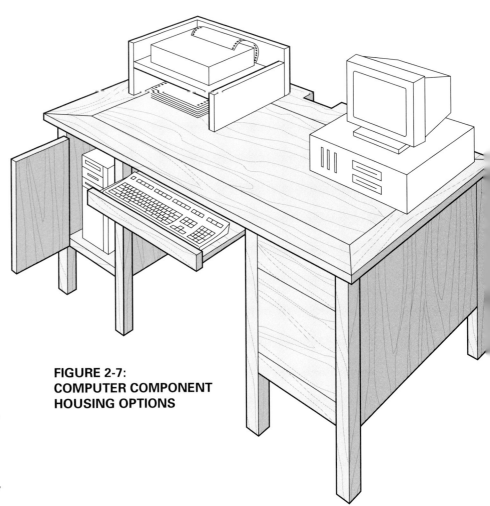

**FIGURE 2-7:
COMPUTER COMPONENT
HOUSING OPTIONS**

frame openings must be wide enough to accept the drawer size you choose.

Not to confuse matters, but files can be placed perpendicular to the drawer facing, so the width can be whatever you like. However, don't make the desk too large. If you have two legal-size pedestal file drawers with commercial slides, the desktop would need to be over 5' long. That's a large desk.

You'll need to allow a bit of clear-ance between the drawer opening and the drawer face. The projects in this chapter have flush drawers, so a special drawer slide, called a fully concealed slide, must be used (see Sources of Supply on page 126 and Cutting Lists on pages 39, 41 and 43). The slides attach to the drawers and the drawer slide cleats. To check for proper fit of all the parts, have the drawer slides on hand before constructing the drawers.

The desk legs are square cut using

your trusty hollow-ground blade on a table saw or radial arm saw. If possible, always work from a planed side when ripping for thickness. Rip the stock slightly oversize and plane back to square on your jointer. If the cut is clean, all you may need to do here is sand to thickness.

All rail and stile stock for the desk base is cut 2½" wide. Refer to the cutting lists for the required lengths.

Several corner joint options are shown in figure 2-8. Biscuits, dowels and the mortise and tenon can be used if the leg is not notched. The stepped-lap and the miter corner joints can be glued and screwed from either the front or back. If you drive screws from the front, be sure to countersink them and cover the holes with wood plugs or buttons.

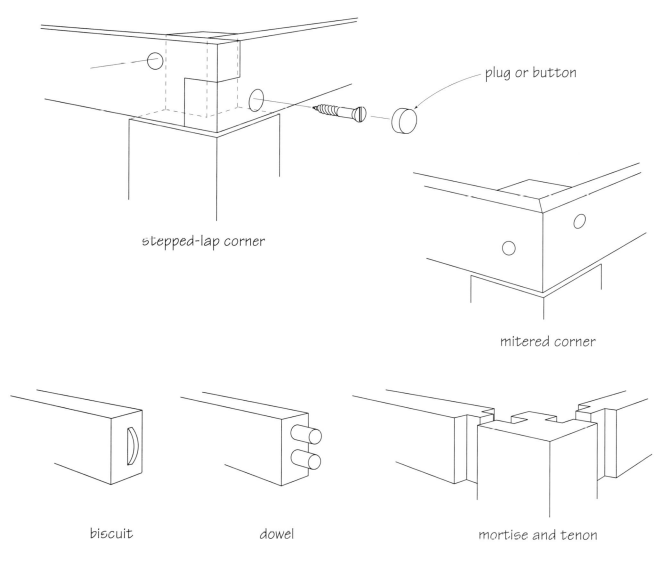

plug or button

stepped-lap corner

mitered corner

biscuit

dowel

mortise and tenon

**FIGURE 2-8:
CORNER JOINTS**

CONSTRUCTION STEPS

STEP 1

Cut Notches for Upper Rails

Cut the legs to length, then use the band saw to cut the notches on the top end of each one. (For the classic-style pedestal desk, make these cuts for both the top and bottom rails.) Refer to the Exploded Views for the location of the notches. If you are making the craftsman-style single-pedestal desk, the front leg on the end brace is notched for the upper rail on one side only.

STEP 2

STEP 2

Cut Notches for Lower Rails

Lay out the locations of the notches for the lower rails, and cut them out with the dado head. Use the miter gauge to support the stock as you make the cut. (This cut isn't required for the classic-style pedestal desk.) On the craftsman-style single-pedestal desk, the front leg on the end brace is notched for the lower rail on one side only.

STEP 3

Cut the Stepped Lap on the Rails

Use a guide fence and a stop to make the first band saw cut, establishing the length and width of the lap. The lap is one-half the rail width, so the blade must be offset from center to allow for the kerf. To complete the lap, make a cross-cut to remove the waste stock. If you are making the mitered rails shown previously in figures 2-5A and 2-6A, use the table saw to cut the 45° miters on each end.

STEP 3

STEP 4

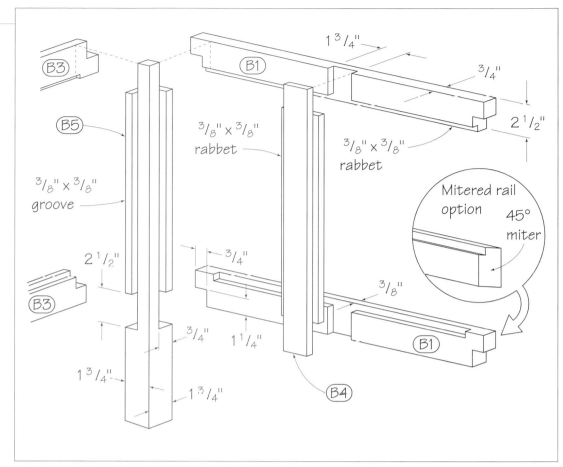

B3

B5

B1

$^3/_8$" × $^3/_8$"
rabbet

$^3/_8$" × $^3/_8$"
rabbet

1 $^3/_4$"

$^3/_4$"

2 $^1/_2$"

$^3/_8$" × $^3/_8$"
groove

Mitered rail
option   45°
miter

2 $^1/_2$"

B3

$^3/_4$"

$^3/_8$"

B1

1 $^3/_4$"

$^3/_4$"

1 $^1/_4$"

1 $^3/_4$"

B4

STEP 5

STEP 4
Study the Construction

A variety of dadoes and grooves are cut in the legs, rails and stiles. Take particular note that the rails have either stopped rabbets or through rabbets. Before making any cuts, it's a good idea to mark the parts to avoid confusion.

STEP 5
Cut the Rail Rabbets

The through rabbet on the rails can be cut with the dado cutter. The stopped rabbet is best cut with a router or, better yet, a router table. The router leaves a rounded corner, so the corner must be cut square with a chisel.

STEP 6

Make the Stile Cuts

Use the dado head to cut the half lap on each end of the stile. Cut the rabbets along each side.

STEP 6

STEP 7

Make the Back Rail Cuts

Lay out the location of the notch and half lap in the upper and lower back rails. Cut them out with the dado head or by making multiple passes with the regular saw blade.

STEP 7

STEP 8

Round the Edges

If you are making the craftsman-style desk, all outside edges, including those on the notches and stepped laps, are rounded to a ¼" radius. The job can be done using a quarter-round bit in the drill press (set to the highest speed), or you can use the router.

STEP 8

STEP 9

Cut and Fit the Panels

Dry assemble the legs, rails and stiles, then measure the opening for the ³/₈"-thick panels. Cut the panels about ¹/₈" narrower than the opening to allow the panel to "float" in the frame. Once cut, check the fit as shown. Oak plywood is used for the panels, but solid stock is an option. However, if solid stock is used, reduce the panel width by an additional ¹/₈". This allows for possible expansion of the panel due to changes in the moisture content of the wood.

As an option, you can use ¹/₂"-thick material for the panels. However, you'll need to cut a ¹/₈"-deep by ¹/₂"-wide rabbet all around each panel in order for the panels to fit in the ³/₈"-wide rabbets and grooves.

Make the Applied Panel

You have the option of embellishing the flat panels by adding an applied panel, resulting in a raised-panel look. The applied panel is shown in figure 2-6A. The applied panel can have angled or coved edges. Coved edges can be cut using the router and a coving bit or with the table saw. To use the table saw, clamp an angled guide across the table and pass the edges of the raised panel over the saw blade diagonally. The radius of the cut will be a function of the saw blade diameter and the angle of the guide. Don't attempt to make the cut in one pass. Instead, make several passes, removing about ¹/₁₆" of stock with each pass.

STEP 10

Assemble the Frames

Use glue and screws to assemble each of the frames. To help keep the frames flat, assemble the parts on a flat surface. Check for squareness before setting the frame aside to dry. If the frame includes side panels, fit them in the grooves and rabbets, then temporarily tack them in place.

STEP 11

Add the Front and Back Rails

Assemble the front rails and the lower back rail, again using glue and screws. If you make the craftsman-style single-pedestal desk, you might not want to glue the back rails in place. Removable back rails make it easier to move the desk, should the need arise.

A combination screw bit makes it easier to drill the holes. The bit bores a countersink, shank and pilot hole in one operation. To keep the corner clean, rails were screwed from the back side. A corner brace, which also serves as a means to attach the top, provides additional strength. As shown in figure 2-8, screws can also be driven from the front, using wood plugs or buttons to fill the countersunk hole.

STEP 12

STEP 13

Install the Back Panels

Add the back panels before the upper back rail is assembled. Also add the slide cleats. The slide cleats not only serve as a means to attach the slides, they also hold the side panels in place. Once the side panels are secured, remove the temporary tacks. The upper back rail can now be added.

STEP 13

STEP 14

Brace the Slide Cleats

A couple of corner braces can be added to help support the slide cleats.

STEP 14

STEP 15

Inset Options

Various options are available for making the center inset for the top. Depending on your setup, you can join the center inset to the frame using any of these options.

STEP 16

Rabbet the Top Inset

The top inset for the craftsman-style desk is made from ½"-thick oak plywood with a rabbet all around the edge. Cut the plywood to length and width, then use the table saw and dado head to cut the rabbet.

STEP 17

Make the Top Sides and Ends

Cut the sides and ends to length and width. Use the dado head or the router table to cut the tenons. Also cut the groove along the inside edge of the sides and ends. Check the parts for a good fit. If all looks OK, add glue to the inset rabbet and to the grooves in the sides and ends. Assemble the parts and clamp firmly with bar or pipe clamps.

If you are making a top with a mitered frame (see figures 2-5A and 2-6A), use biscuits, dowels or splines to reinforce the miter joint.

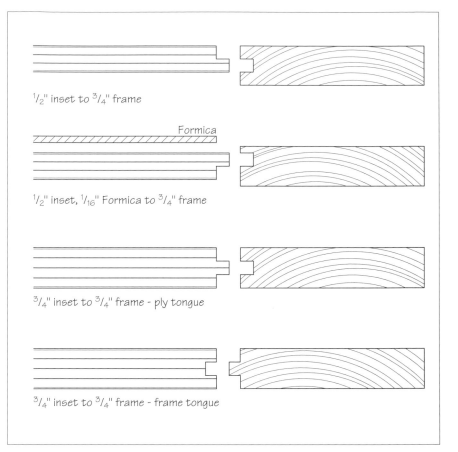

½" inset to ¾" frame

Formica

½" inset, ¹⁄₁₆" Formica to ¾" frame

¾" inset to ¾" frame - ply tongue

¾" inset to ¾" frame - frame tongue

STEP 15

STEP 16

STEP 17

STEP 18

Add the Top and Drawers

Center the top on the base, then drive screws through the cleats and corner braces into the underside of the top. Don't use glue here if you want to be able to "knock down" the desk in the future. As an option, commercial tabletop fasteners can be used in place of the cleats. Most mail-order companies carry them (see Sources of Supply on page 126). You'll need to either rout a groove or biscuit-cut a mating slot in the upper rails to receive the tab end of the fastener.

The drawers for this project are described in chapter seven, including the keyboard tray in lieu of the kneehole drawer. Drawer dimensions for the various pedestal desk drawers are shown in figures 2-4A, 2-5A and 2-6A.

If you plan to use commercial drawer slides with the flush drawers shown, fully concealed slides must be used. They are available from The Woodworker's Store (see Sources of Supply on page 126 and Cutting Lists on pages 39, 41 and 43). Of course, as an option, you can mount the drawers on wooden slides as shown in the chapter one projects.

The keyboard uses computer desk slides, also available from The Woodworker's Store. Mounting brackets allow these slides to be attached to the underside of the top. A 1/4"-thick spacer cleat (not shown in the exploded view) may be needed to install the slides flush with the underside of the top ends and sides (see chapter seven, page 115, center).

CHAPTER THREE

SECRETARY DESKS

The projects in this chapter offer all sorts of design possibilities. The styles can range from an enclosed-top cabinet and base to the open-face country-style secretary on legs. The doors can be either glazed or paneled, or you can do without them entirely. The base can be a combination of drawers and doors. A fold-down writing surface is shown on the enclosed versions of the secretary. A pigeonhole organizer (shown in the country-style organizer, chapter eight), can be customized to meet your writing needs.

If you build the secretary on legs or enclose only the sides and back, the hinged slant-front panel is optional. The kneehole below the desk opens more design opportunities, especially on a vertical fall-front design, which could include vertical or horizontal tamboured cover, or even hinged doors forming a triptych when opened.

Consider building the cupboard base and bookcase as separate units, as detailed in the traditional secretary desk. Separate pieces become more practical as the size of the project increases. Also the two-piece approach is probably a little easier to build.

The classic secretary was built from premium veneer plywood. A 4' x 8' sheet of dimensionally stable plywood is well suited for larger furniture such as this, but either of the other construction methods in this book would work. For example, the country-style secretary, made from solid pine, might better suit your needs.

Classic details make this walnut secretary an exceptionally fine piece of furniture.

Secretary Desks

CLASSIC SECRETARY DESK

This piece has fairly simple lines and few embellishments. It is made from ³/₄"-thick walnut veneer plywood, but any premium veneer plywood would work. As with any plywood, exposed edges need to be capped. The shape of the cap edges can vary depending on location and function. Wider caps, such as those around the bookcase, desk area and cabinet, also serve as casings.

Paneled glass doors are shown for the bookcase, but these could be single-pane doors, a wire grill or wood panels. The leaded glass option is reserved for the traditional secretary desk, which is more ornate.

The desk cabinet contains the slant-front writing surface, a single drawer, and a cupboard behind a pair of frame-and-panel doors. The base rests on corner feet built up from one-by stock.

FIGURE 3-1: CLASSIC SECRETARY DESK

TRADITIONAL SECRETARY DESK

As the name suggests, this desk has a more traditional look. The caps stand proud of side panels to provide added relief and an opportunity to add moulding details. The moulding could be a cove or quarter-round, but feel free to use any moulding profile that suits your tastes.

The desk is shown on a full base with ogee feet, but it could be raised on cabriole or turned legs if the upper cabinet is shortened, as in the country-style secretary desk. The upper cabinet is shown with a broken pediment and appropriate finial. Another option is to cut a fairly deep cove around the top and base to reflect a period design.

FIGURE 3-2:
TRADITIONAL
SECRETARY DESK

COUNTRY-STYLE SECRETARY DESK

The country-style secretary desk is designed to be easier to build. It shows how a secretary desk can be built on a leg base. The cabinet does not have doors. The country style could become Shaker style with very little adaptation.

Maple or birch veneer plywood would look good here, or perhaps a painted desk made from ordinary, but quality, plywood would fit this design. For the inside back panel, a tongue-and-groove, shiplap or beaded board pattern, reminiscent of earlier times, would look good.

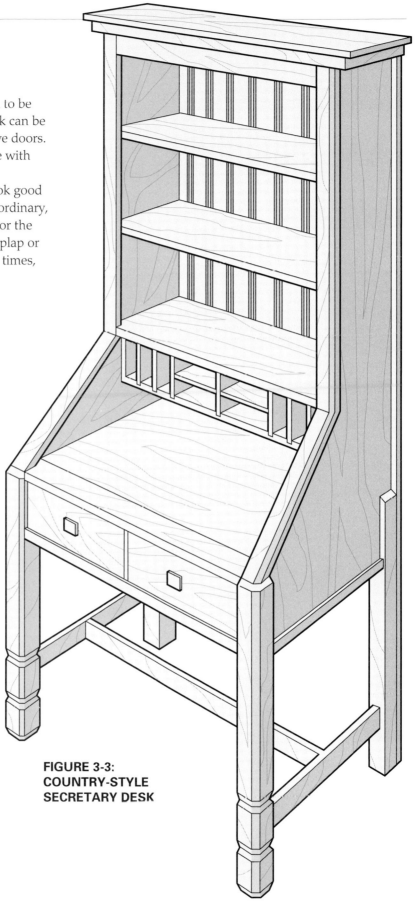

**FIGURE 3-3:
COUNTRY-STYLE
SECRETARY DESK**

Classic Secretary Desk
DIMENSIONS

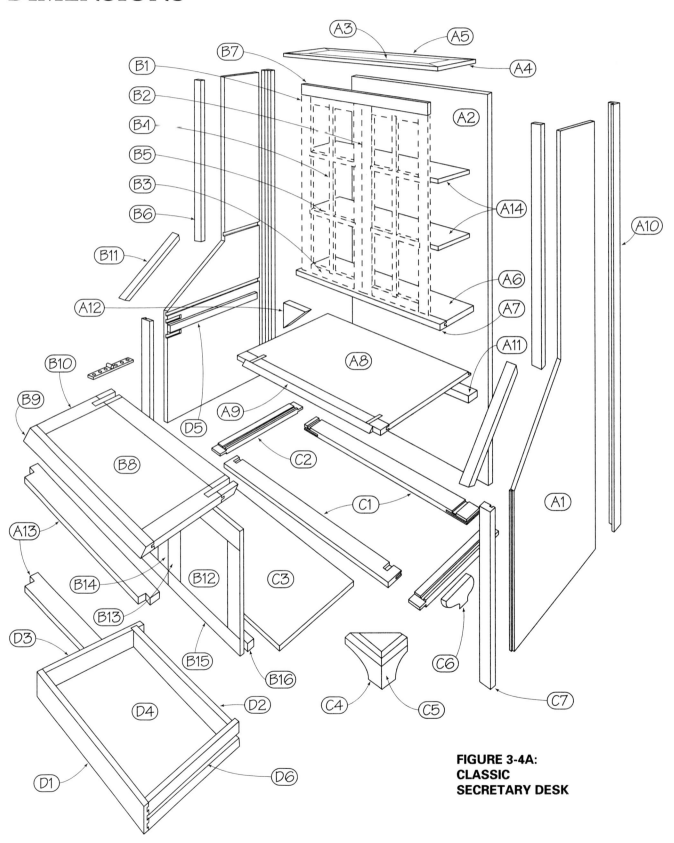

FIGURE 3-4A:
CLASSIC
SECRETARY DESK

CUTTING LIST—CLASSIC SECRETARY DESK

Case

(A1)	Side	(2)	$^3/_4$" x $20^1/_2$" x 66"*	Plywood
(A2)	Back		$^1/_2$" x $28^3/_4$" x 66"	Plywood
(A3)	Top		$^3/_4$" x $10^3/_4$" x $30^1/_4$"**	Plywood
(A4)	Top Cap (End)	(2)	$^3/_4$" x $^3/_4$" x $10^3/_4$"	Walnut
(A5)	Top Cap (Front/Back)	(2)	$^3/_4$" x $^3/_4$" x $31^1/_4$"	Walnut
(A6)	Bookshelf Base		$^3/_4$" x $9^1/_4$"*** x $28^3/_4$"	Plywood
(A7)	Bookshelf Base Cap		$^3/_4$" x $^3/_4$" x $28^3/_4$"	Walnut
(A8)	Desk Shelf		$^3/_4$" x 19"*** x $28^3/_4$"	Plywood
(A9)	Desk Shelf Cap		$^3/_4$" x $1^1/_2$" x $28^3/_4$"	Walnut
(A10)	Narrow Side Cap	(2)	$^3/_4$" x 1" x $65^3/_4$"	Walnut
(A11)	Desk Shelf Support		$^3/_4$" x 3" x $28^1/_4$"	Walnut
(A12)	Gusset	(2)	$^3/_4$" x 4" x 4"	Walnut
(A13)	Front Stretcher	(2)	$^3/_4$" x 3" x $28^3/_4$"	Walnut
(A14)	Shelf	(2)	$^3/_4$" x 9" x $28^1/_4$"	Walnut

Upper Doors

(B1)	Stile	(3)	$^3/_4$" x $1^1/_2$" x $30^3/_8$"	Walnut
(B2)	Stile (Center/Left)		$^3/_4$" x $1^3/_4$" x $30^3/_8$"	Walnut
(B3)	Rail	(4)	$^3/_4$" x $1^1/_2$" x $13^3/_8$"	Walnut
(B4)	Stile Muntin	(2)	$^3/_4$" x $^3/_4$" x $28^1/_8$"	Walnut
(B5)	Rail Muntin	(4)	$^3/_4$" x $^3/_4$" x $11^1/_8$"	Walnut
(B6)	Side Cap	(2)	$^3/_4$" x $1^1/_2$" x $31^7/_8$"	Walnut
(B7)	Lintel		$^3/_4$" x 1" x $27^1/_4$"****	Walnut

Slant Door

(B8)	Panel		$^3/_4$" x $11^1/_4$" x $24^1/_4$"**	Plywood
(B9)	Cap (Front/Back)	(2)	$^3/_4$" x $1^1/_2$" x $26^3/_4$"	Walnut
(B10)	Cap (End)	(2)	$^3/_4$" x $1^1/_2$" x $11^1/_4$"	Walnut
(B11)	Side Cap	(2)	$^3/_4$" x $1^1/_2$" x $14^3/_4$"	Walnut

Lower Door

(B12)	Panel	(2)	$^3/_4$" x $10^7/_8$" x $15^1/_4$"**	Plywood
(B13)	Stile	(3)	$^3/_4$" x $1^1/_2$" x $17^3/_4$"	Walnut
(B14)	Stile (Center/Left)		$^3/_4$" x $1^3/_4$" x $17^3/_4$"	Walnut
(B15)	Rail	(4)	$^3/_4$" x $1^1/_2$" x $10^7/_8$"****	Walnut
(B16)	Doorstop		$^3/_4$" x $^3/_4$" x $28^1/_4$"	Walnut

Base

(C1)	Front/Back	(2)	$^3/_4$" x $2^1/_4$" x $28^1/_2$"*****	Walnut
(C2)	End	(2)	$^3/_4$" x $2^1/_4$" x 22"	Walnut
(C3)	Bottom		$^1/_2$" x 18" x 28"	Plywood
(C4)	Front Foot (Face)	(2)	$1^1/_2$" x $3^1/_2$" x 6"	Walnut
(C5)	Front Foot (Side)	(2)	$1^1/_2$" x $3^1/_2$" x 6"	Walnut
(C6)	Back Foot	(2)	$1^1/_2$" x $3^1/_2$" x 6"	Walnut
(C7)	Side Cap	(2)	$^3/_4$" x $1^1/_2$" x 24"	Walnut

Drawer

(D1)	Face		$^3/_4$" x $3^3/_4$" x $26^3/_4$"	Walnut
(D2)	Back		$^3/_4$" x $3^3/_4$" x $24^3/_4$"	Alder
(D3)	Side	(2)	$^3/_4$" x $3^3/_4$" x 18"	Alder
(D4)	Bottom		$^1/_8$" x 17" x $24^3/_4$"	Masonite
(D5)	Slide Cleat	(2)	$^3/_4$" x $3^3/_4$" x $19^1/_4$"	Alder
(D6)	Slide	(2)	$^7/_8$" x $1^3/_4$" x $18^1/_2$"	Accuride

* Width includes $^3/_8$"-long tongues
** Length and width includes $^1/_4$"-long tongues
*** Width includes $^1/_4$"-long tenons
**** Length includes $^1/_4$"-long tongues
***** Length includes $^1/_2$"-long tongues

NOTES

1. Material specified as plywood is walnut veneer plywood.

2. Drawer slides and slant-door hinges available from The Woodworker's Store (see Sources of Supply on page 126).

3. Desk shelf width allows for extra stock. Trim as needed to fit.

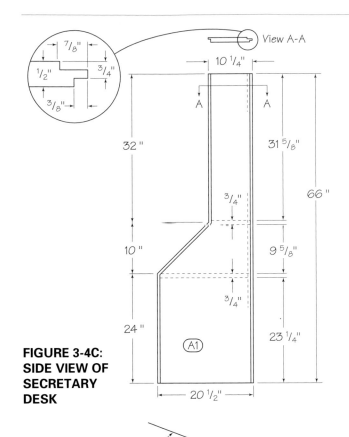

**FIGURE 3-4C:
SIDE VIEW OF
SECRETARY
DESK**

View A-A

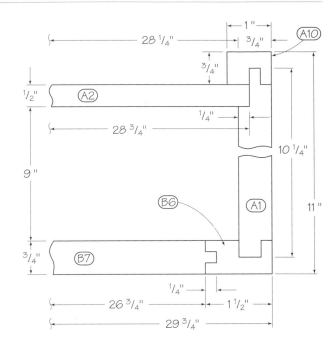

**FIGURE 3-4D:
TOP VIEW OF UPPER CASE**

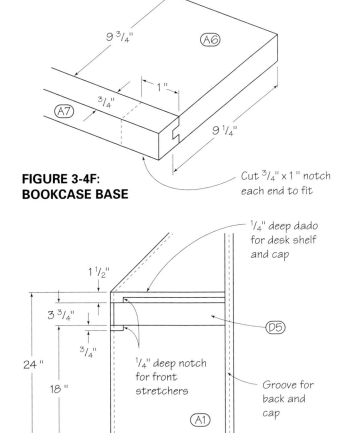

**FIGURE 3-4F:
BOOKCASE BASE**

Cut ³/₄" x 1" notch
each end to fit

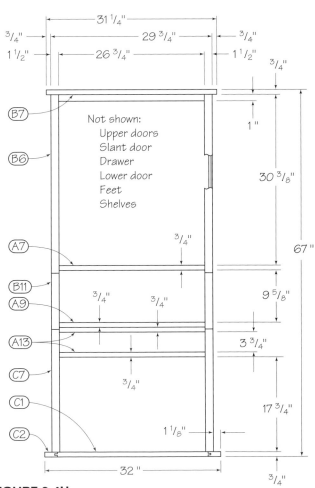

¹/₄" deep dado
for desk shelf
and cap

¹/₄" deep notch
for front
stretchers

Groove for
back and
cap

Not shown:
Upper doors
Slant door
Drawer
Lower door
Feet
Shelves

**FIGURE 3-4G
SIDE VIEW OF CASE WITH
DRAWER ASSEMBLY**

**FIGURE 3-4H:
FRONT VIEW OF BASE CASE**

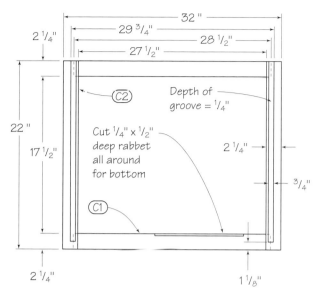

FIGURE 3-4E:
TOP VIEW OF BASE FRAME

Depth of groove = 1/4"

Cut 1/4" x 1/2" deep rabbet all around for bottom

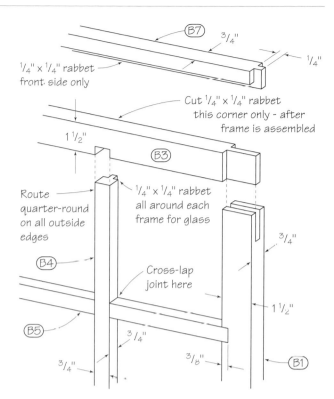

1/4" x 1/4" rabbet front side only

Cut 1/4" x 1/4" rabbet this corner only - after frame is assembled

1/4" x 1/4" rabbet all around each frame for glass

Route quarter-round on all outside edges

Cross-lap joint here

FIGURE 3-4J:
UPPER DOOR DETAIL

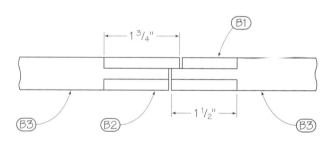

FIGURE 3-4K:
TOP VIEW OF UPPER DOOR

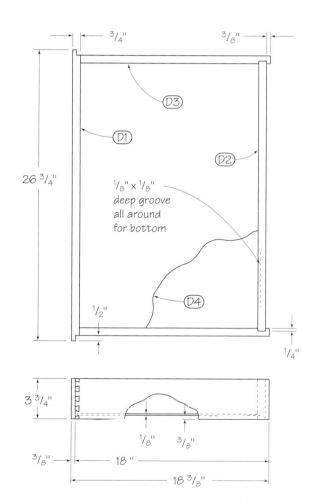

1/8" x 1/8" deep groove all around for bottom

FIGURE 3-4I:
DRAWER DETAIL

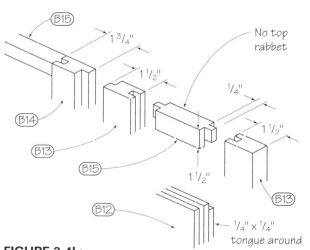

No top rabbet

1/4" x 1/4" tongue around

FIGURE 3-4L:
LOWER DOOR JOINTS

Traditional Secretary Desk
DIMENSIONS

TOP VIEW OF UPPER CASE

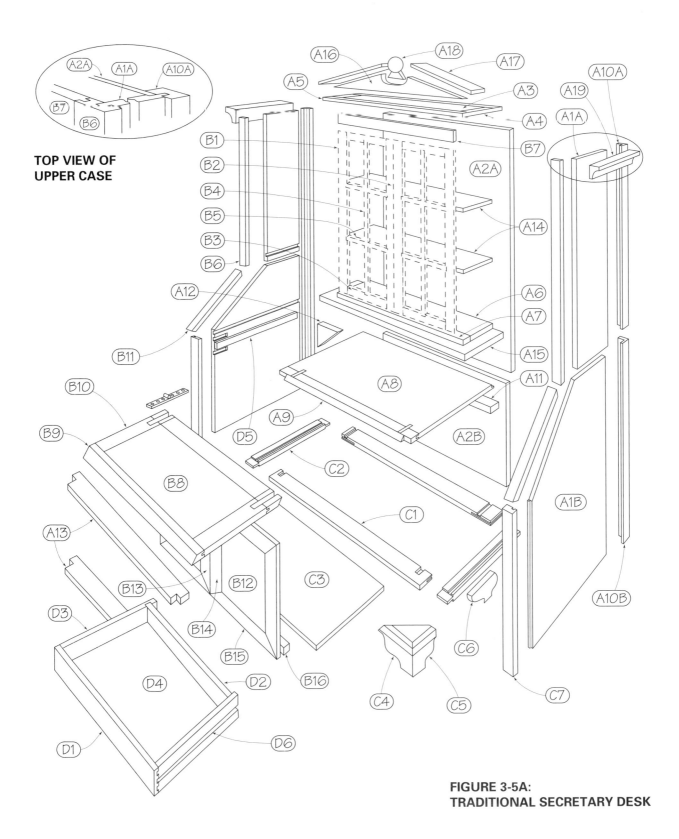

FIGURE 3-5A:
TRADITIONAL SECRETARY DESK

CUTTING LIST—TRADITIONAL SECRETARY DESK

Two-Piece Case

(A1A) Upper Side	$3/4$" x $10^1/4$" x $32^7/8$"*	Plywood
(A1B) Lower Side	$3/4$" x $20^1/2$" x $33^7/8$"*	Plywood
(A2A) Upper Back	$1/2$" x $28^3/4$" x $32^7/8$"	Plywood
(A2B) Lower Back	$1/2$" x $28^3/4$" x $33^5/8$"	Plywood
(A3) Bookshelf Top	$3/4$" x 11" x $30^3/4$"**	Plywood
(A4) Top Cap (End) (2)	$3/4$" x $3/4$" x 11"	Maple
(A5) Top Cap(Front/Back) (2)	$3/4$" x $3/4$" x $31^3/4$"	Maple
(A6) Bookshelf Base	$3/4$" x $9^1/4$"*** x $28^3/4$"	Plywood
(A7) Bookshelf Base Cap	$3/4$" x $3/4$" x $28^3/4$"	Maple
(A8) Desk Shelf	$3/4$" x 19"*** x $28^3/4$"	Plywood
(A9) Desk Shelf Cap	$3/4$" x $1^1/2$" x $28^3/4$"	Maple
(A10A) Narrow Side Cap	$3/4$" x $1^1/4$" x $32^5/8$"	Maple
(A10B) Narrow Side Cap	$3/4$" x $1^1/4$" x $33^3/8$"	Maple
(A11) Desk Shelf Support	$3/4$" x 3" x $28^1/4$"	Maple
(A12) Gusset (2)	$3/4$" x 4" x 4"	Maple
(A13) Front Stretcher (2)	$3/4$" x 3" x $28^3/4$"	Maple
(A14) Shelf (2)	$3/4$" x 9" x $28^1/4$"	Maple
(A15) Lower Case Top	$3/4$" x 11" x 32"	Maple
(A16) Pediment Face	$3/4$" x $3^1/2$" x 30"	Maple
(A17) Pediment Top (2)	$3/4$" x 3" x 15"	Maple
(A18) Finial	$2^1/2$" x $2^1/2$" x 5"	Maple
(A19) Moulding (3)	$7/8$" x $1^1/2$" x as needed	Maple

Upper Doors

(B1) Stile (3)	$3/4$" x $1^1/2$" x $30^3/8$"	Maple
(B2) Stile (Center/Left)	$3/4$" x $1^3/4$" x $30^3/8$"	Maple
(B3) Rail (4)	$3/4$" x $1^1/2$" x $13^3/8$"	Maple
(B4) Stile Muntin (2)	$3/4$" x $3/4$" x $28^1/8$"	Maple
(B5) Rail Muntin (4)	$3/4$" x $3/4$" x $11^1/8$"	Maple
(B6) Side Cap (2)	$3/4$" x $1^3/4$" x $32^5/8$"	Maple
(B7) Lintel	$3/4$" x $1^1/2$" x $27^1/4$"****	Maple

Slant Door

(B8) Panel	$3/4$" x $11^1/4$" x $24^1/4$"**	Plywood
(B9) Rail (2)	$3/4$" x $1^1/2$" x $26^3/4$"	Maple
(B10) Stile (2)	$3/4$" x $1^1/2$" x $13^3/4$"	Maple
(B11) Side Cap (2)	$3/4$" x $1^3/4$" x $14^3/4$"	Maple

Lower Door

(B12) Panel (2)	$3/4$" x $10^7/8$" x $15^1/4$"**	Plywood
(B13) Stile (3)	$3/4$" x $1^1/2$" x $17^3/4$"	Maple
(B14) Stile (Center/Left)	$3/4$" x $1^3/4$" x $17^3/4$"	Maple
(B15) Rail (4)	$3/4$" x $1^1/2$" x $13^3/8$"	Maple
(B16) Doorstop	$3/4$" x $3/4$" x $28^1/4$"	Maple

Base

(C1) Front/Back	(2)	$3/4$" x $2^1/4$" x $28^1/2$"*****	Maple
(C2) End	(2)	$3/4$" x $2^1/4$" x 22"	Maple
(C3) Bottom		$1/2$" x 18" x 28"	Plywood
(C4) Front Foot	(2)	$1^1/2$" x $3^1/2$" x 6"	Maple
(C5) Side Foot	(2)	$1^1/2$" x $3^1/2$" x 6"	Maple
(C6) Back Foot	(2)	$1^1/2$" x $3^1/2$" x 6"	Maple
(C7) Side Cap	(2)	$3/4$" x $1^3/4$" x 24"	Maple

Drawer

(D1) Face	1" x $3^3/4$" x $26^3/4$"	Maple
(D2) Back	$3/4$" x $3^3/4$" x $24^3/4$"	Alder
(D3) Side (2)	$3/4$" x $3^3/4$" x 18"	Alder
(D4) Bottom	$1/8$" x 17" x $24^3/4$"	Masonite
(D5) Slide Cleat (2)	$3/4$" x $3^3/4$" x $19^1/4$"	Alder
(D6) Slide (2)	$7/8$" x $1^3/4$" x $18^1/2$"	Accuride

    * Width includes $3/8$"-long tongues
    ** Length and width includes $1/4$"-long tongues
    *** Width includes $1/4$"-long tenons
    **** Length includes $1/4$"-long tongues
    ***** Length includes $1/2$"-long tongues

NOTES

1. Material specified as plywood is maple veneer plywood.

2. Drawer slides and slant-door hinges available from The Woodworker's Store (see Sources of Supply on page 126).

3. Widths for desk shelf and lower case top allow for extra stock. Trim as needed to fit.

4. Front of drawer face is beveled on all four edges.

5. Stiles and rails for slant door and lower door are mitered. Mitered joints are reinforced with biscuits.

6. Notch top end of parts B6 and A10A to allow for moulding.

7. See figure 3-4E on page 61 for base frame construction.

8. See figure 3-4F on page 60 for bookcase base construction.

9. See figure 3-4I on page 61 for drawer construction (except use 1" stock for face).

10. See figures 3-4J and 3-4K on page 61 for upper door construction.

11. See figure 3-4L on page 61 for lower door construction.

Country-Style Secretary Desk
DIMENSIONS

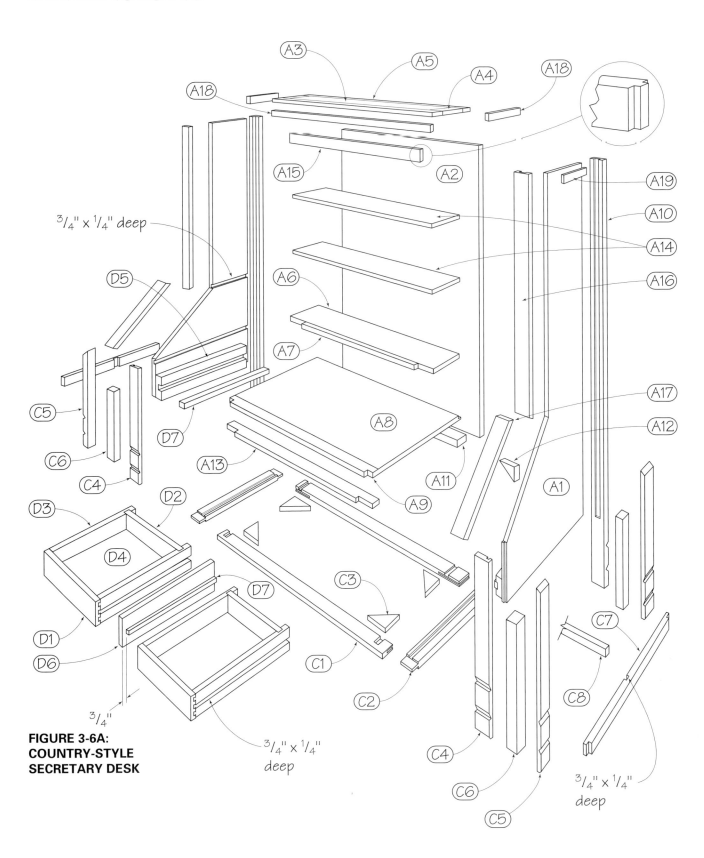

$^3/_4$" × $^1/_4$" deep

$^3/_4$"

$^3/_4$" × $^1/_4$" deep

$^3/_4$" × $^1/_4$" deep

**FIGURE 3-6A:
COUNTRY-STYLE
SECRETARY DESK**

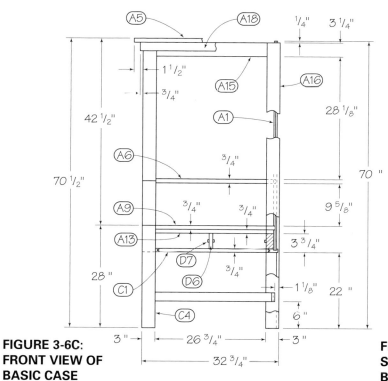

FIGURE 3-6C:
FRONT VIEW OF
BASIC CASE

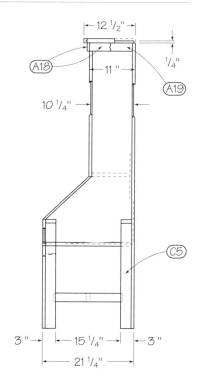

FIGURE 3-6D:
SIDE VIEW OF
BASIC CASE

CUTTING LIST—COUNTRY-STYLE SECRETARY DESK

Case

(A1) Side	(2)	$^3/_4$" x $20^1/_2$" x $47^1/_2$"*	Plywood
(A2) Back		$^1/_2$" x $30^1/_4$" x $47^1/_2$"	Plywood
(A3) Bookshelf Top		$^3/_4$" x $11^1/_2$" x $34^3/_4$"**	Plywood
(A4) Top Cap (End)	(2)	$^3/_4$" x $^3/_4$" x $11^1/_2$"	Alder
(A5) Top Cap (Front/Back)	(2)	$^3/_4$" x $^3/_4$" x $35^3/_4$"	Alder
(A6) Bookshelf Base		$^3/_4$" x $9^1/_4$"*** x $30^1/_4$"	Plywood
(A7) Bookshelf Base Cap		$^3/_4$" x $^3/_4$" x $30^1/_4$"	Alder
(A8) Desk Shelf		$^3/_4$" x $18^3/_4$" x $30^3/_4$"	Plywood
(A9) Desk Shelf Cap		$^3/_4$" x $1^1/_2$" x $30^1/_4$"	Alder
(A10) Side Cap	(2)	$^3/_4$" x 3" x $69^3/_4$"	Alder
(A11) Desk Shelf Support		$^3/_4$" x $1^1/_2$" x $29^3/_4$"	Alder
(A12) Gusset	(2)	$^3/_4$" x 4" x 4"	Alder
(A13) Stretcher		$^3/_4$" x 3" x $29^3/_4$"	Alder
(A14) Shelf	(2)	$^3/_4$" x 9" x $29^3/_4$"	Alder
(A15) Lintel		$^3/_4$" x $3^1/_4$" x $27^1/_4$"****	Alder
(A16) Side Cap	(2)	$^3/_4$" x 3" x $32^1/_8$"	Alder
(A17) Side Cap	(2)	$^3/_4$" x 3" x $15^1/_2$"	Alder
(A18) Trim	(2)	$^3/_4$" x 2" x as needed	Alder
(A19) Trim End Filler	(2)	$^3/_4$" x 2" x $9^1/_2$"	Alder

Base

(C1) Front/Back	(2)	$^3/_4$" x $2^1/_4$" x $28^1/_2$"*****	Alder
(C2) End	(2)	$^3/_4$" x $2^1/_4$" x $21^1/_4$"	Alder
(C3) Corner Brace	(4)	$^3/_4$" x 4" x 4"	Alder
(C4) Leg Face	(2)	$^3/_4$" x 3" x 28"	Alder
(C5) Leg Side	(4)	$^3/_4$" x $2^1/_4$" x 28"	Alder
(C6) Leg Filler Block	(4)	$2^1/_4$" x $2^1/_4$" x 22"	Alder
(C7) Side Brace	(2)	$^3/_4$" x 2" x 16"*	Alder
(C8) Cross Brace		$^3/_4$" x 2" x $29^1/_2$"	Alder

Drawer

(D1) Face	(2)	$^3/_4$" x $3^3/_4$" x 13"	Alder
(D2) Back	(2)	$^3/_4$" x $3^3/_4$" x 12"	Alder
(D3) Side	(4)	$^3/_4$" x $3^3/_4$" x 18"	Alder
(D4) Bottom	(2)	$^1/_8$" x 12" x 17"	Masonite
(D5) End Guide	(2)	$1^1/_2$" x $3^3/_4$" x $19^1/_4$"	Alder
(D6) Center Guide		$^3/_4$" x $3^3/_4$" x 20"	Alder
(D7) Runner	(4)	$^3/_4$" x $^3/_4$" x $19^1/_4$"	Alder

    * Width includes $^3/_8$"-long tongues
   ** Length and width includes $^1/_4$"-long tongues
  *** Width includes $^1/_4$"-long tongues
 **** Length includes $^1/_4$"-long tenons
***** Length includes $^1/_2$"-long tenons

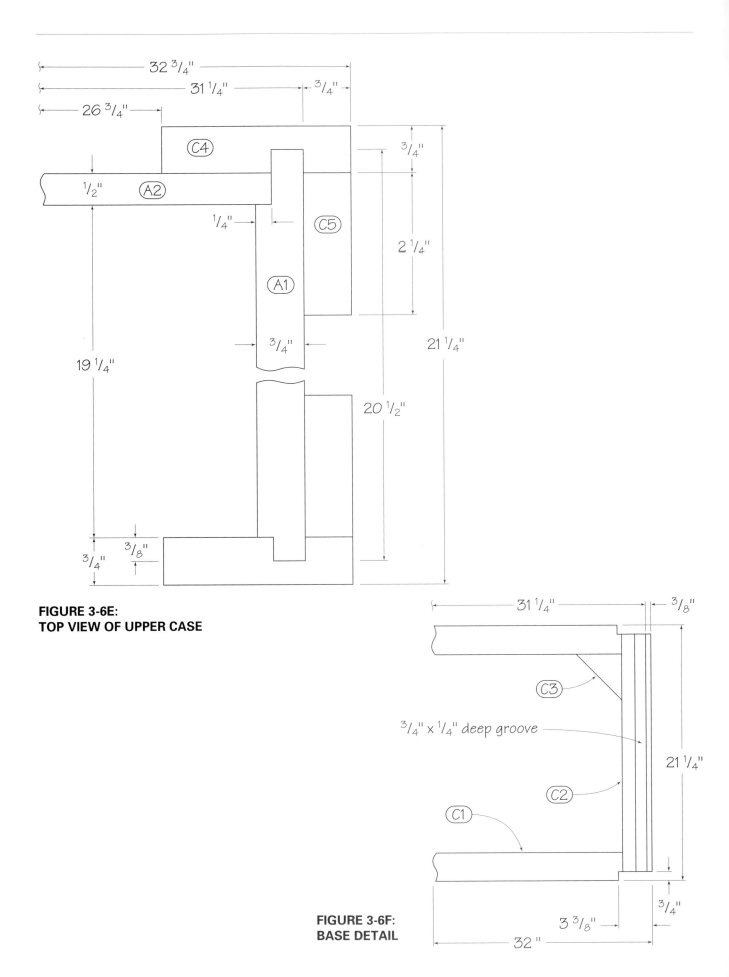

FIGURE 3-6E:
TOP VIEW OF UPPER CASE

FIGURE 3-6F:
BASE DETAIL

Secretary Desks
CONSTRUCTION NOTES

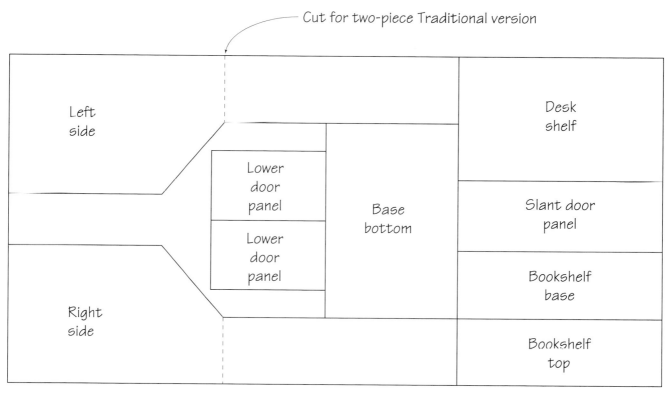

Cut for two-piece Traditional version

Left side

Lower door panel

Lower door panel

Base bottom

Right side

Desk shelf

Slant door panel

Bookshelf base

Bookshelf top

$^3/_4$" ply - Secretary - Classic and Traditional versions

**FIGURE 3-7:
CUTTING LAYOUT**

Even though walnut veneer plywood was selected for the classic secretary desk, solid stock or frame-and-panel construction might better suit your particular needs. I chose plywood because of the project size. A pair of 4' x 8' plywood sheets netted the parts for the desk. You'll find that ½"-thick and ¾"-thick veneer plywood are available in several wood species, including walnut, oak and cherry.

Figures 3-7, 3-7A and 3-7B show cutting layouts in order to net the maximum pieces from 4' x 8' plywood sheets. The diagram above shows ¾"-thick, two-sided veneer (sides A and B). The back and bottom of the desk (figure 3-7A on page 68) are cut from a sheet of ½" plywood. If ½" plywood isn't available locally, you can glue ¼" plywood back-to-back, as I did. However, the imported ¼" plywood I used actually measured ³/₁₆" thick. It's best to measure the thickness before cutting any dado or rabbet joints for the plywood.

Since a 4' x 8' plywood sheet is unwieldy, cut the plywood into easier to manage pieces using a portable saber saw or circular saw. Use a hollow-ground or plywood finishing blade for a smooth cut.

Even after reducing these pieces to the smallest possible sizes, you still might need some auxiliary support for the final trimming. Table extensions or a good helper make the effort easier.

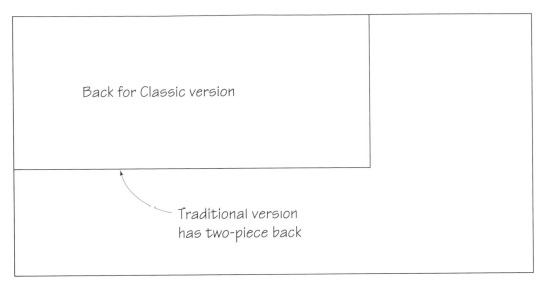

½" ply or double thickness ¼" ply

FIGURE 3-7A:
CUTTING LAYOUT

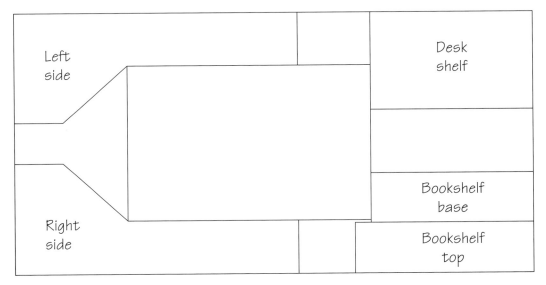

¾" ply - Secretary - Country version

FIGURE 3-7B:
CUTTING LAYOUT

The first cut is across the 66" height. Don't rip down the center. Do the layout first, then cut out the left and right sides.

When building the traditional desk, which has a separate top case, crosscut 32" down for the bookcase sides. Mark the adjoining boards if you want a contiguous figuring pattern.

Square-cut the top and bottom of the bookshelf and the work surface pieces. If larger than your table saw setup, use the auxiliary fence method described in chapter one. Set the remaining parts aside while you work the sides.

Ordinarily, cap stock has a tongue that fits into grooves cut in the plywood, but in this secretary

desk, some of the plywood is covered with wide cap stock, so it is more practical to groove the caps and cut tongues on the plywood.

If using a jointer to plane the narrow cap stock, cut a matching tongue in 3"- or 4"-wide scrap plywood to hold the thin cap as it's passed over the cutter.

STEP 1

STEP 1

Cut the Sides

Rip the bookshelf depth to 10¼" back to the slant, 32" down from the top. Stop ripping well before the slant front angle, and finish the cut with hand or portable saw. By cutting the bookcase depth first, you net more remaining material for shelves and door panels. Trim back the cabinet base sides to 20½".

The photo shows an auxiliary fence clamped to the plywood. This is the angled cut for the slant front, but all the pieces could be cut using this method. There's no reason you can't get a true cut using a plywood blade on your saber saw or a hollow-ground blade on a portable circular saw.

To position the auxiliary fence parallel to the cut, clamp a fence offset by the distance between the inside edge of the kerf and the guide edge on your portable saw. Use your depth gauge or set your combination square to this distance.

Also at this time, cut the ¼"-deep by ¾"-wide dadoes for the bookcase shelf and the desk shelf.

STEP 2

Consider the Cap Options

All exposed plywood edges need an applied cap to give the edges a finished look. A few options are shown here. The cap can be as simple as an edging veneer, available in rolls or sheets. Some manufacturers impregnate this product with hot glue so it can be applied with an electric iron. A clean cut is the only prerequisite for a good edge. Any overhang can be trimmed or sanded flush to the edge.

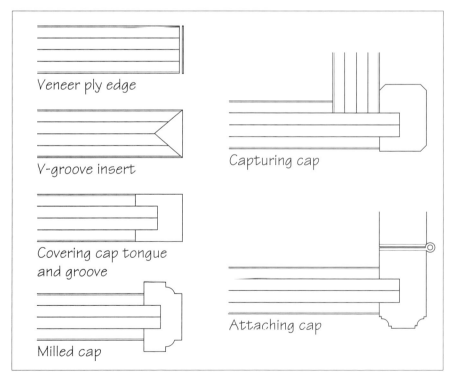

Veneer ply edge

V-groove insert

Covering cap tongue and groove

Milled cap

Capturing cap

Attaching cap

STEP 2

STEP 3

Consider the Corner Joint Options

In plywood case construction, you can eliminate edge caps by mitering, dadoing or rabbeting the corners. Corners can be mitered (and maybe splined) to fully cover the plywood edge. Dado grooves can be cut just inside the edge (inset in the back for instance) so only one of the two edges is left exposed. You can also rabbet (with or without a dado) close to the veneer layer to reduce or eliminate core exposure.

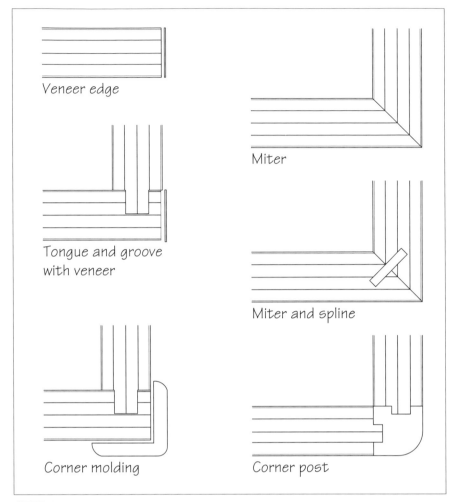

Veneer edge

Tongue and groove with veneer

Corner molding

Miter

Miter and spline

Corner post

STEP 3

STEP 4

Cut Tongues on Side Edges

Using a router and an auxiliary fence (a yardstick will do), cut the tongue along the front and back edges of the sides. The top and bottom edges do not have a tongue. The tongue along the back edge is cut deeper to allow for the back. Also cut the ¼"-deep notches for the stretchers.

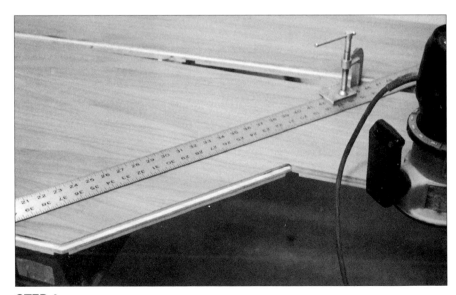

STEP 4

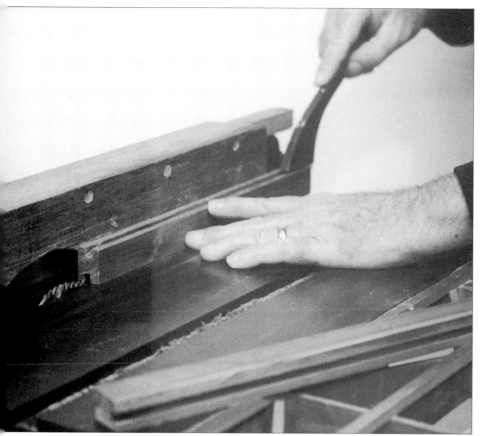
STEP 5

Rough-Cut Edge Caps

Select stock for the cap edging. Look for interesting color and grain, and keep a mental note of the intended placement. Rip the stock slightly wide so it can be planed smooth to the final width.

Dado the grooves to match the tongues cut into the plywood. Position the groove so the cap is at or proud of the veneered surface. The parts should fit snugly for a solid glue joint. In areas subject to stress, such as the caps that double as a door case, the glue joints should be augmented with corner cleats or decorative angles.

If you are using $3/4$" x $3/4$"-wide edge caps (or less), dado both sides of wide stock, then rip the stock into two lengths to the desired thickness.

STEP 6

Make the Base

The same base is used for all three secretary desks, although the base for the country-style version isn't as wide. If you plan to have an extra-hefty coving all around the base, cut the front, back and ends a bit wider.

Note that the ends have a $1/4$"-deep by $3/4$"-wide groove to accept the bottom end of the sides. Stop the dado short of the face, then square the rounded corner with a wood chisel. The edge caps cover this part, so clearance, not perfection, is your objective.

After the frame is assembled, use the router and a piloted rabbeting bit to cut a $1/4$"-wide by $1/2$"-deep rabbet all around the inside edge for the bottom. Square the rounded corners with a chisel. The bottom can be added later.

STEP 7

Assemble Base to Sides

Temporarily screw the sides into the dado groove of the base. Don't use glue at this time. This early assembly lets you check and fit other parts as you proceed.

STEP 7

STEP 8

Add the Desk Shelf

Cut the top, the bookcase base and the desk shelf to length. Cut the desk shelf wider than needed. The front and rear edges will be worked later.

Clamp the desk shelf in place between the sides. Add a pipe clamp across the back and front to hold the parts together.

STEP 8

STEP 9

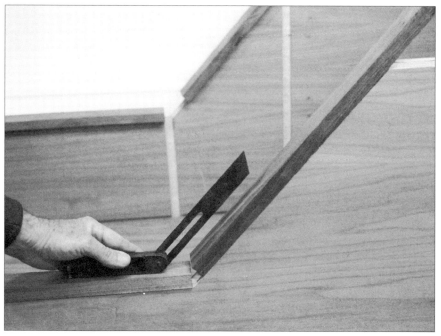

STEP 10

Make the Top

Cut the top to length and width, then cut the ¼"-deep dadoes to accept the sides. Cut a ¼"-wide by ¼"-long tongue all around the edge of the top. Also use the router to cut the ¼"-deep groove for the back.

Next, cut the cap edging for the top. The corners may be mitered or butt joined. If butt joined, glue the ends first and allow them to dry. Then recut the tongue across the newly affixed ends. Glue the front and back caps in place. Where the edging protrudes into the groove, chisel back to let in the vertical sides.

Cut Side Caps

At the front edge of the sides, the wider edge caps also form the door frames and the casing for the slanted cover. These can be added early in the assembly so you are not forever handling bits and pieces. Interior parts will be installed through the back, which is added after the shelves and the slant front are fitted.

Miter the joints above and below the slant front. Bisect these angles and mark each piece using an adjustable square. If you don't cut a miter joint, one piece is going to overlap another, thereby exposing end grain. Exposed end grain might look good in certain designs but not this one.

STEP 11

Assemble the Side Caps

With all pieces duly fit and finish sanded, glue and clamp the wide caps to the mating plywood edges. When clamping, be sure the facings remain square to the plywood sides and parallel to the base.

STEP 12

Add Angled Clamp Blocks

To clamp the slanted edge caps, angled blocks are cut to provide a clamping surface for the pipe clamps. This procedure helps apply good, even clamp pressure to the caps. Make the blocks from extra cap stock. The cap stock has matching dado grooves so it fits snugly on the edge tongue.

STEP 13

Clamp the Slanted Caps

Add the pipe clamps, and tighten to apply pressure. If an angled block tends to slide, place a C-clamp (use clamp pads) just above the block to keep it in place.

STEP 11

STEP 12

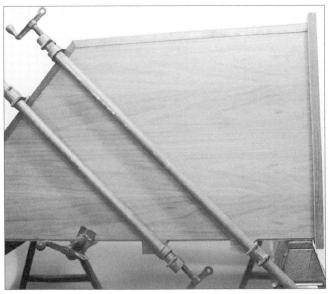

STEP 13

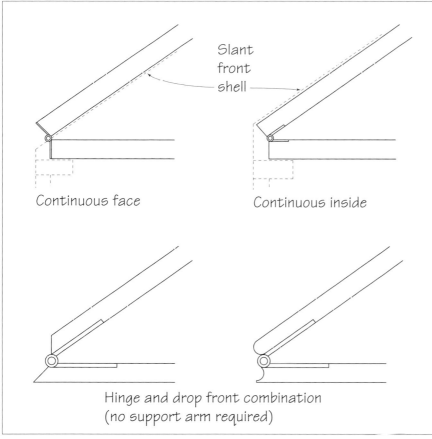

Slant front shell

Continuous face

Continuous inside

Hinge and drop front combination
(no support arm required)

STEP 14

STEP 15

Hinge Options

A hinge joint connects the desk shelf and slant door. At the hinge joint, the edge shape of the desk shelf and slant door is dictated by the hinge style you choose. The edges can be square-cut, angled or rounded. A few hinge options are shown.

Cut the Bevels

Cut and assemble the parts for the slant door. The top and bottom edges should be cut a bit wider than necessary to allow for the beveling cuts. By the way, the slant door frame would ordinarily be a candidate for mitered corners, but in deference to the bevels, the long members run the width of the opening. By this time, the desk shelf should be cut to width, but it's going to need a cap to match the mating part on the slant door.

For the hinge style I used, a 45° angle was cut after the caps were applied to the plywood panel. You could precut this angle by ripping the 45° angle down the center of a wider board, then dadoing the ripped edge to match the plywood tongue of the desk shelf and slant cover. The same procedure is used to cut the upper bevel of the slant door flush along the bookshelf base.

Final Fit Desk Shelf and Slant Door

In this design, the desk shelves are flush with the cap. If this is your design as well, notch the corners to clear the front frame. Also bevel the shelf where the slanted-face frame interferes.

NOTE

A cover designed to the full width of the secretary (on top of the desk sides) can be hinged closer to the face. If inset (like the example), the hinge pin must be inset from the frame so the cover is flush with the flanking frame.

Make the Desk Hinge Template

The installation of the hinge/support/arm hardware you are using for this project is next. The following discussion pertains to the drop hinges installed in the classic secretary desk.

No matter what kind of hardware you use, the hinges should be mortised flush with the surfaces. For the secretary hinges, this involves routing a fairly long (4") dado in both the desk shelf and the slant door.

Prepare a template for the router. Install a guide bushing and a straight bit (about $\frac{1}{4}$" diameter) in your router. The distance from the outside diameter of the guide bushing to the router bit is the distance the template should be enlarged to net the shape of the hinge strip. Use a compass or pair of dividers to trace the hinge shape, plus the added allowance for the routing guide.

STEP 17

STEP 18

Cut the Desk Hinge Mortise

Test the template size and cutting depth on a piece of scrap stock. When all looks OK, clamp routing template in place. Make sure it is aligned and inset the proper distance, then mortise to the depth of the hinge.

STEP 19

Cut the Hinge Barrel Recess

Chisel a small secondary mortise to accept the barrel of the hinge. This cut allows the hinge to be fully recessed.

STEP 20

Dry Fit the Slant Door

Add the slant door, and check it for squareness and fit. Trim the sides as necessary, and verify that the top bevel on the door butts to the bookshelf base. You may want to add a stop inside the cabinet as a rest for the slanted cover.

STEP 21

Install Stretchers

Because the desk shelf is set back from the cap, add the upper front stretcher to the case. The stretcher supports the desk shelf along the hinge line, and it also serves as the top casing for the drawer below. The lower front stretcher can also be added now. Both the upper and lower stretchers fit into notches cut earlier in the sides. Also, the stretchers are notched to fit flush with the front cap.

In addition, add the desk shelf support and gussets under the back of the desk shelf. This piece provides added support at the back.

STEP 21

STEP 22

Add Drawer Slides

Screw the side cleats to the inside of the case. When installed, the side cleats must be flush with the cap edging. The drawer slides are then attached to the side cleats.

Also at this point, give some thought to how you will support the two shelves. You can use commercial track (shelf standards) or cleats, or simply drill a series of holes to receive shelf tabs.

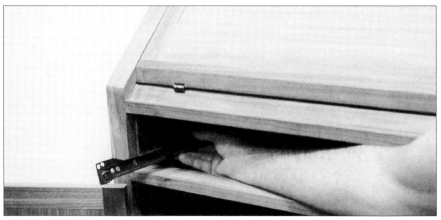

STEP 22

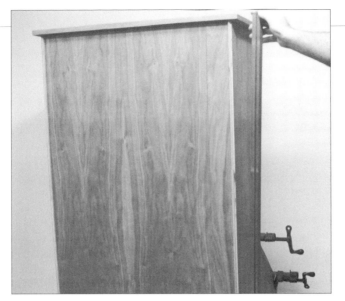

STEP 24

STEP 23
Attach the Back

The back is let into the rabbets cut earlier in the sides. It is held in place by the narrow side caps. To ensure that the case is square and aligned while the glue is setting, tack the corners in place. The caps are cut to length and glued in place after the top is added.

After the caps are dry, add a ³/₄"-thick by 3"-wide support cleat (not shown on the drawing) across the back and between the cap edges. Locate the cleat so that it can be screwed to the back edge of the desk shelf. A couple of gussets under the brace add further support. The cleat not only adds strength, it provides a convenient place to grip the case when it must be lifted and moved.

STEP 24
Install the Lintel

The lintel fills in the door opening and provides a strike plate for the upper doors. To create the strike plate, a rabbet is cut the full length of the lintel and along the top edge of the upper doors.

STEP 25
Attach the Top

This top has been on and off the assembly so many times there should be no problem finally gluing it in place. If you don't have long pipe clamps that span the length of the case, add corner gussets or cleats to provide a clamping surface for a few shorter clamps.

STEP 25

Install Lower Doors

Make the lower doors, and check to see how they fit on the case. The jointer can be used if any trimming is needed. To avoid tearing out the end-grain stock while jointing, first make a short cut through the end grain of the stile on one end. Then turn the door and make a full pass from the opposite end of the door. (Because the first end is undercut, the jointer blades can run out the other end on the second pass without tearing the end grain.)

The procedure for making, fitting, glazing and hanging the upper doors is explained in chapter six. Chapter seven tells you how to make the drawer.

STEP 26

Cut the Feet

Cut a foot base frame or independent corner feet, as shown here. The classic secretary desk has feet built up from ³/₄"-thick stock. The more ornate ogee foot used on the traditional secretary desk is cut from 2"-thick stock.

STEP 27

STEP 28

Scribe the Arc

Use a template or a compass to scribe the curve on each foot. Cut out the curve with a band saw. The two halves of each front foot are joined using a miter and spline joint.

STEP 29

Add Base and Feet

The base can now be permanently glued and screwed to the base. Once the base is installed, use glue and screws to attach the feet. Note the use of glue blocks to reinforce the joint. When the feet are assembled, add glue to the rabbet cut earlier in the base and install the bottom panel.

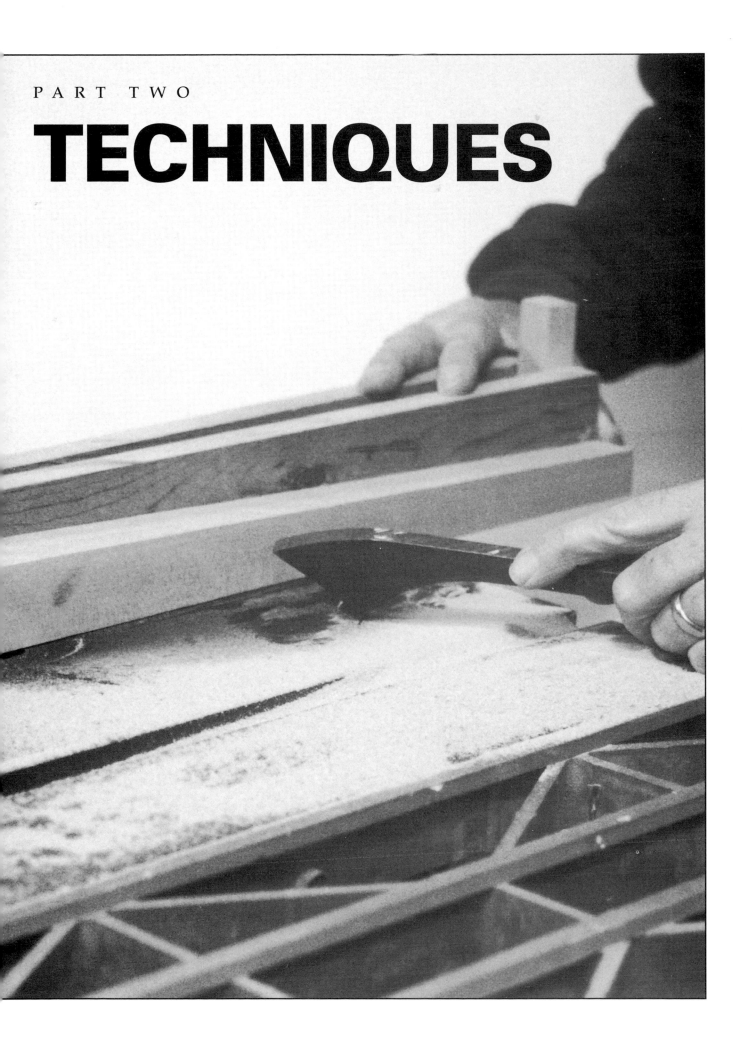

PART TWO

TECHNIQUES

Techniques

In part two, I'm supposed to divulge the wisdom of the workshop, but I suspect you already know many of the things I will discuss. Maybe, however, I picked up a trick or technique you missed along the way.

Woodworking is a pleasure, no matter what your skill level. There are favorite tasks and least favorite tasks, but the process is always challenging and the results never fail to be rewarding.

TOOLS

Your workshop and the tools you put in it are a reflection of you as a woodworker. Tools can often indicate the kind of projects you build, the amount of time you spend in your shop and your passion for the hobby of woodworking.

Some woodworkers use only hand tools, others only portable power tools. A fortunate group have workshops equipped with almost every hand tool, portable power tool and stationary machine you can imagine.

Of course, no workshop is ever complete. There is always the process that could be aided by a specialty tool. A miter cutoff saw comes to mind. When cutting a batch of moulding lengths for what seems like a thousand framed panels, such a tool would be handy. If what you do offers many opportunities to amortize this saw, it probably should be in your arsenal.

Even the lack of simple tools can be frustrating. A rabbeting plane, for example, would have been helpful in building these projects. Why, after years of building and writing about boat projects, I haven't acquired a rabbeting plane is a mystery—an inexcusable oversight. While working on this book, a search for a spokeshave turned up nothing in the shop (I'm sure Dad had one at one time); it would have come in handy when forming the sample cabriole leg. Enough griping, I should go buy what I need.

RECOMMENDED TOOLS

If you have the available space, a table saw or a radial arm saw belongs in your workshop. If space is a problem, a portable circular saw (Skilsaw) or a saber saw can suffice as your primary tool, but portable circular and saber saws are more useful supplementing the larger power saws.

A couple of types of saw blades can help you get the most out of your table saw or radial arm saw. A combination blade does a good job ripping and crosscutting, while a fine-tooth blade is best to use when cutting Plexiglas or plywood. In addition, an expandable dado blade or a wobble blade will come in handy for cutting dadoes, grooves or rabbets.

A 4" belt sander is among the "musts" for your workshop, along with a high-speed portable palm or orbital sander. Each of these tools can help smooth things over nicely.

Another essential tool is the portable router. With a good selection of router bits, the router can cut dovetails, rabbets, dadoes, grooves, moulding and veins. It can also mill sticking, shape edges and more.

A sharpening wheel or belt is needed to keep a keen edge on chisels, plane blades and turning tools. A carborundum wheel will put a fine edge on your cutting tools.

A drill belongs in your basic tool collection. A variable-speed, reversible type is a good choice. This tool not only makes it easy to drill holes, it does a great job driving screws. The cordless models are handy for the shop, as well as for site work.

OPTIONAL TOOLS

Although the band saw is versatile, it is not a do-it-all tool. However, with a good selection of blades, you can resaw, crosscut, rip and miter. You can even cut tenons and produce scroll work.

The lathe is a rewarding tool and one that I personally enjoy (even though there is a definite shortage of turnings in this book).

A drill press is mostly used to drill holes, but it can also be used as an overhead router. This tool might even belong in the recommended category.

The scroll saw is perfect for cutting scroll work, inlays, marquetry and the like.

CHAPTER FOUR

JOINERY

Woodworkers can choose from a wide variety of joints, and volumes have been written about the many joinery techniques. The joint you select is determined by such factors as design, application, function, strength, stability and lateral forces. Joints that you enjoy making, as long as they do the job, are likely to be used most often.

A variety of woodworking joints are discussed in this book. They include

- Butt Joints
- Edge Joints
- Doweled Edge Joints
- Milled Edge-Gluing Joints
- Rabbet Joints
- Dado Joints
- Biscuit Joints
- Mortise-and-Tenon Joints
- Lap Joints
- Miter Joints
- Finger (or Box) Joints
- Dovetail Joints (through, blind, half-blind, slip)

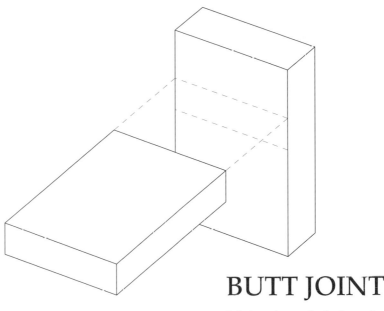

**FIGURE 4-1:
BUTT JOINT**

BUTT JOINT

Joining the end of a board to the surface of another creates a butt joint. This is the easiest joint to make. However, since end grain offers little glue strength, this joint must be reinforced. Dowels, splines, biscuits, screws, corner blocks and gussets are among the various methods used to strengthen butt joints.

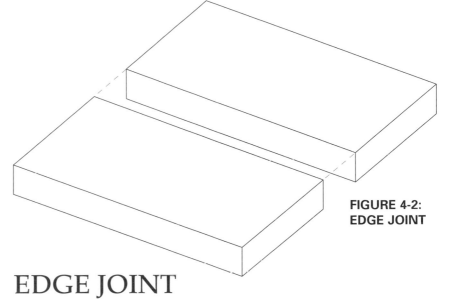

**FIGURE 4-2:
EDGE JOINT**

EDGE JOINT

Unlike butt joints, edge joints mate the long-grain surfaces of boards. When two long-grain surfaces are properly glued, the resulting joint is stronger than the wood itself.

DOWELED EDGE JOINT

The addition of dowels to an edge joint helps keep the boards aligned during glue-up. Chapter one provides a detailed explanation of this procedure.

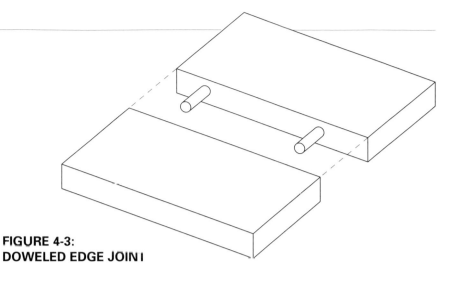

FIGURE 4-3:
DOWELED EDGE JOINT

MILLED EDGE-GLUING JOINT

You can cut a glue-joint profile in the edges of boards with a router bit, shaper cutter or moulding-head cutter. The special interlocking profiles provide additional glue area and help keep the edges aligned when clamp pressure is applied. The profile shown is called a straight glue joint, but other profiles are also available. If you don't want to buy a special set of bits, you can simply cut a tongue-and-groove joint.

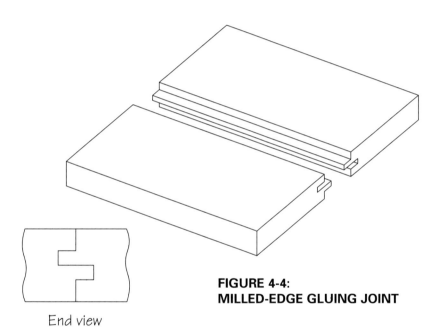

End view

FIGURE 4-4:
MILLED-EDGE GLUING JOINT

RABBET JOINT

A groove cut into the end or edge of a board creates a rabbet, a joint that has many woodworking applications. Rabbet joints are commonly used to construct drawers, drawer frames and boxes.

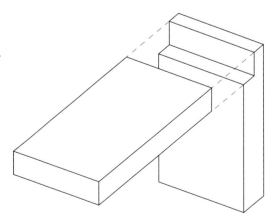

FIGURE 4-5:
RABBET JOINT

DADO JOINT

A groove cut across the grain of a board is called a dado joint. It is used to join the end of one board to the surface of another. When the groove is cut parallel to the grain direction, the cut is called a groove joint.

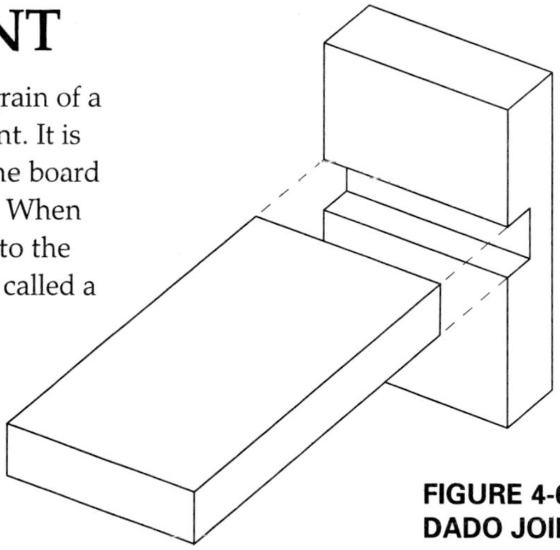

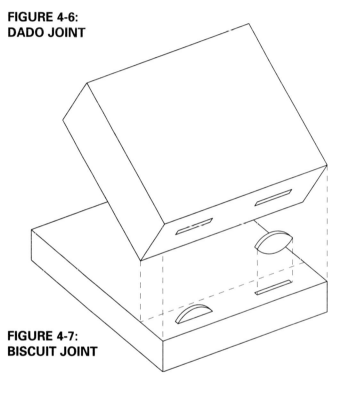

FIGURE 4-6:
DADO JOINT

BISCUIT JOINT

A biscuit joiner or a router with a biscuit-cutting attachment can make butt joints a breeze. Working from a common surface, all cuts are equidistant from the flush edge. The biscuits fit into the radius of the biscuit cutter. This is possibly the least painful method to join butted edges.

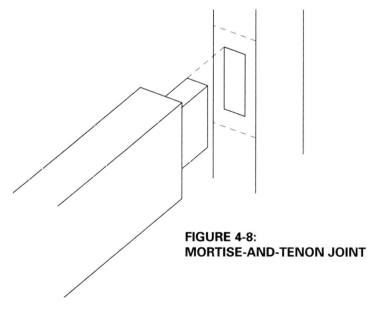

FIGURE 4-7:
BISCUIT JOINT

MORTISE-AND-TENON JOINT

The mortise and tenon is one of the strongest joints for connecting two boards that meet at right angles. The size of the mortise and tenon depends on the stock size and the application. Several versions of the mortise and tenon are shown in chapter one.

FIGURE 4-8:
MORTISE-AND-TENON JOINT

LAP JOINT

Removing one half the thickness from two mating boards allows them to overlap with both face surfaces flush. The end lap joint is shown, but various other lap joints can be cut.

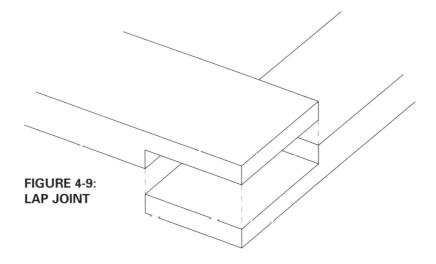

FIGURE 4-9: LAP JOINT

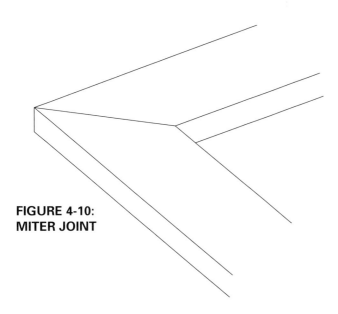

FIGURE 4-10: MITER JOINT

MITER JOINT

Joining two boards at an angle creates a miter joint. This joint is generally used to conceal the end grain of the boards.

FINGER (OR BOX) JOINT

The interlocking fingers create considerable gluing area, making this an especially strong joint.

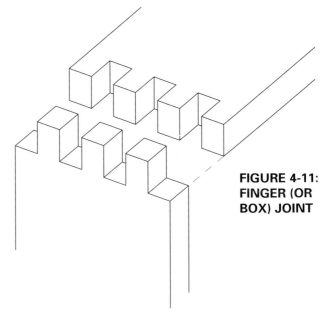

FIGURE 4-11: FINGER (OR BOX) JOINT

DOVETAIL JOINT

The dovetail is not only exceptionally strong, it is one of the most attractive of all the woodworking joints. This joint is strong because of the generous gluing area and the mechanical strength provided by the wedge-shape dovetails. It is often used in drawer construction.

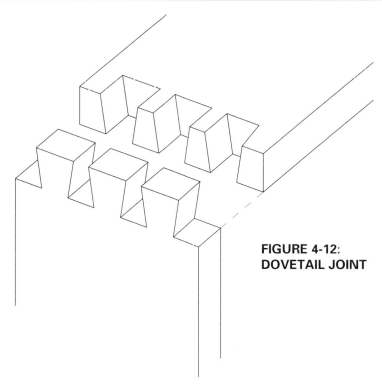

**FIGURE 4-12:
DOVETAIL JOINT**

MECHANICAL FASTENERS

Sometimes, a mechanical fastener offers the best joinery option. A wide variety of mechanical fasteners are at your service. They include wood screws, self-cutting screws, finishing nails, carriage bolts, threaded inserts and turnbuckles, to name a few.

When fastening with wood screws, be sure the pieces are well butted in place. Don't rely on regular wood screws to bring the pieces home. Self-cutting, dry-lubricated wood screws do a better job and are great in production assembly, especially when using homoge-

neous compositions such as MDF (medium density fiberboard).

When using wood screws, combination bits are great time-savers. In one operation, a combination bit bores the shank, pilot and countersink holes. Combination bits are available in sizes that match standard screw sizes.

You can get a good idea of the many mechanical fastener options by poking through mail-order woodworking catalogs or woodworking retail stores. Don't hesitate to ask for advice.

CHAPTER FIVE

LEGS

As they say, nothing beats a good pair of legs or, in this case, two pairs of legs that complement the design. Legs are often the focal point of a furniture design, so it's important they look good. The legs should be well proportioned and match the overall design of the piece.

Of course, the legs must also be sturdy because they support the entire weight of the desk. However, that doesn't mean all legs have to look clunky. A well-designed leg can provide plenty of strength, yet look surprisingly light and delicate.

This chapter includes several leg styles, along with details explaining how to make the tapered leg for the writing desk shown in chapter one, figure 1-1. If you don't like tapered legs for this project, consider straight-sided, right-angled corner legs (see chapter one, figure 1-3), suitable for a taller lectern desk

(standing or podium height), with cross braces to stiffen the structure.

Turned legs are yet another option. The turnings can be tapered, cylindrical or beaded. Shy away from the heavy look for this piece. Avoid the use of claw feet.

The cabriole leg, with its graceful curves, adds an elegant look to the writing desk shown in chapter one, figure 1-2. However, this leg is going to require somewhat more time and effort to build. If you like the style but don't want to make them, you can purchase ready-made cabriole legs (see Sources of Supply on page 126).

There are two bracket-foot designs used with the secretary desks in chapter three. A straight-sided version is shown in figure 3-1, while figure 3-2 features an ogee profile. Both add a nice detail to the projects.

TAPERED LEGS

The writing desk shown in chapter one, figure 1-1, has legs that are tapered on all four sides. Each taper starts 5″ from the top end of the leg and measures 22″ long. The bottom end of the leg measures 1″ square (see figure 5-1).

The tapered legs can be made in several ways. You can scribe the lines of the taper on each leg, then cut to the lines with a sharp hand plane; or you can use the band saw to cut just outside the scribed lines, then use a hand plane to cut exactly to the line. Tapered legs can also be cut on the jointer, and if you have a table saw, tapers can quickly be cut using a tapering jig. That's the method I used.

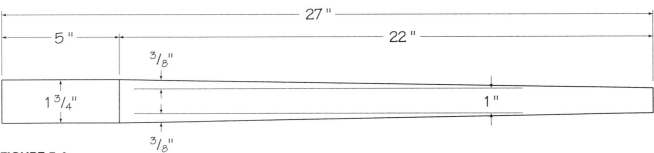

FIGURE 5-1:
TAPERED LEG

STEP 1

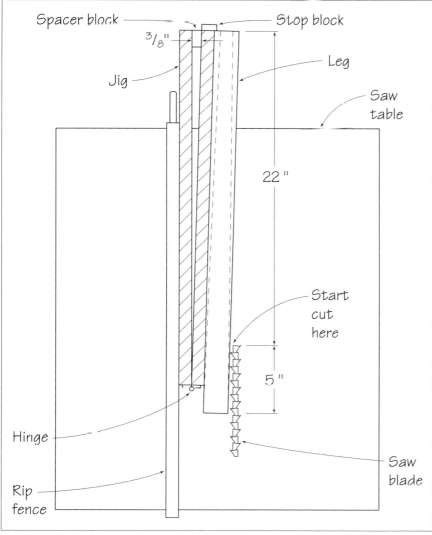

STEP 2

STEP 1

Make the Tapering Jig

Tapering jigs can be purchased from just about any retail or mail-order store that sells woodworking supplies (see Sources of Supply on page 126), or, as shown, you can make a simple tapering jig. It consists of two straight boards joined at one end with a hinge. At the other end, a stopblock and spacer block are attached. (The size of the spacer block varies depending upon the angle of the taper you cut.) The jig holds the leg stock at the correct angle as the stock is passed through the saw blade. Both the stock and the tapering jig are advanced together as a unit along the rip fence. It's a good idea to use a push stick to hold the leg securely in place, and always keep your fingers a safe distance from the saw blade.

A clean, sharp, hollow-ground blade is going to give you the smoothest cut. If a jointer is to follow, cut the tapers $1/32$" thicker on each cut, then plane the four edges down to the final thickness.

STEP 2

Set Up the Jig Cut

To make the leg shown in figure 5-1, cut a $3/8$" spacer block and secure it to the jig. Then with the jig and leg in position, locate the rip fence so that the saw blade will begin its cut at a point 5" from the top end of the leg. Check the taper angle (spacer length) by measuring the distance offset from blade to stock at the end of the taper run.

STEP 3

Make the First and Second Taper Cuts

With the leg butted against the stopblock, make the first tapering cut. If a full-thickness cut is too much for your saw, make the cut in two passes. Make the first pass with the blade height equal to about one-half the leg thickness. Then raise the blade to the full thickness, and make a second pass to complete the cut.

After the first taper is cut, make the second taper on an adjacent side of the leg. Don't make the second cut on the side opposite the first cut.

STEP 4

Make the Third and Fourth Taper Cuts

Replace the $\frac{3}{8}$" spacer block with a $\frac{3}{4}$" block. Now, with one of the previously tapered sides against the jig, make the third cut. Then to complete the tapers, make the fourth and final cut.

STEP 5

Smooth the Legs

Sand all four of the legs through 220-grit. A stationary belt sander, if you have one, comes in handy here. A few light passes with a sharp hand plane also does the job nicely.

STEP 4

STEP 5

STEP 6

Break the Corners

Secure the leg in a vise, and break the sharp corners using a hand plane or sandpaper. For a more defined detail, you might bevel the corners using the jointer or a hand plane.

STEP 7

Embellishments (Optional)

If you like, various embellishments can be added to the legs. You can break the edges with a half-round groove or facet the corners. Also, the tapers and the upper faces can be decorated with veining details. It's your project, so feel free to let your imagination guide you.

TURNED LEGS

If you prefer turned legs for the writing desks in chapter one, many viable design options are available. You can achieve the same profile of the square taper by turning the stock from 1¾" down to 1" within 22", or, as shown in figure 5-9A, you can turn a beading detail just below the 5"-long square section. Also note the shallow cove detail across the square section of the turning.

You can also embellish the square legs on the pedestal desk by turning a separate bottom section and pegging it to the leg as shown in figure 5-9B.

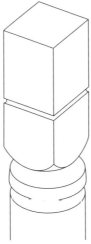

FIGURE 5-9A

Option
Turn spindle legs separately with ³/₄" dia. x ¹/₂" peg to glue into square leg

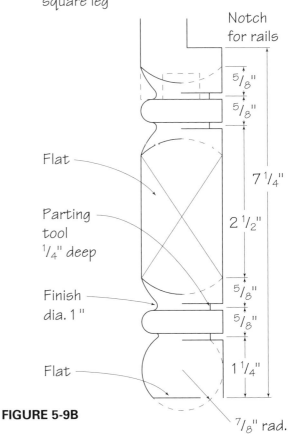

Notch for rails

⁵/₈"

⁵/₈"

Flat

7¹/₄"

Parting tool ¹/₄" deep

2¹/₂"

Finish dia. 1"

⁵/₈"

⁵/₈"

Flat

1¹/₄"

⁷/₈" rad.

FIGURE 5-9B

CABRIOLE LEGS

Cabriole legs can be rough-cut and rounded by hand using a drawknife, wood rasps and files. The outer convex surface can be turned on your lathe. The inside concave profile is cut using a band saw or saber saw. This becomes an eccentric piece, so work has to be turned and tooled slowly. As mentioned earlier, if you prefer not to make these legs, ready-made cabriole legs are available (see Sources of Supply on page 126).

To cut blanks for a Queen Anne or other cabriole designs, draw the front view on the face of square stock and the profile view 90° to the face. First cut the two flanking sides defining the face-on view. It is helpful to use thicker stock than needed so spoilage from the band saw cut is left intact after being cut away. Temporarily tape or tack these pieces back in place to square up the piece, then cut the 90° inside profile.

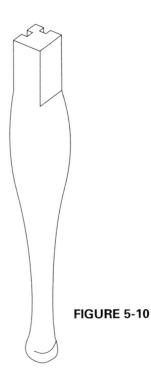

FIGURE 5-10

RIGHT-ANGLED LEGS

The podium height lectern desk lends itself to a simple right-angled leg. For added support, the legs are cross braced front to back, with a stretcher spanning the lower cross braces. Another option is to add a low brace spanning the back legs. A forward brace could be added, but it would interfere with your feet and prohibit bellying up to the high desk on a tall stool.

Joinery options include the mortise and tenon, dowel pins or dovetail crosspieces. Another approach is to cross-lap the legs and aprons where they intersect. Braces can be screwed to the inside faces of the legs.

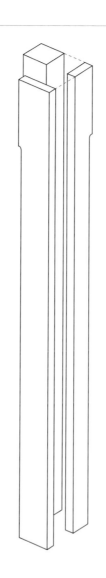

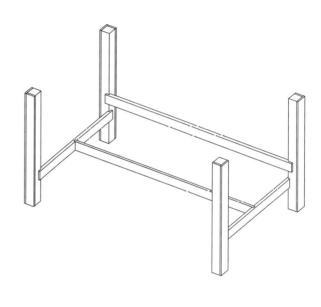

TURNED SEGMENTS

The turned legs for the desk shown in chapter two, figure 2-2, are made from one long piece of stock. However, as an option, you can turn a short length of stock for each leg. Each short length, called a segment, is then doweled to a length of square stock to create the full-length leg.

BRACKET FOOT

Straight-sided bracket feet are used for the secretary desk in chapter three, figure 3-1. These feet are not difficult to make, and they add a nice detail. Ogee (curved) bracket feet are used for the secretary desk shown in figure 3-2.

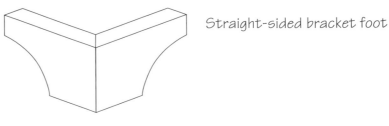

Straight-sided bracket foot

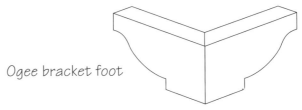

Ogee bracket foot

BRACKET FOOT TEMPLATE

A template can be used to duplicate arcs in the front and side members of the bracket feet. Whether cutting the straight-sided version or the more ornate ogee, a template helps guide the way.

CUTTING THE BRACKET-FOOT OGEE

A band saw with a fairly deep throat is a must for cutting the ogee bracket foot. The stock is held on end to make the curved cut.

CUTTING THE MITER

Set the band saw miter gauge to 45°, then cut the miters on the front and side members of each bracket. After the miters are cut, the bracket parts are joined with splines and supported with an angle brace. The brace connects to the bottom with dowel pins and long wood screws.

END MOULDING OPTION

As an option, a moulding can be applied along each side of the secretary desk at the ogee foot base. Use glue and small countersunk finishing nails to secure the moulding. Countersink each of the finishing nails, then fill the holes with wood putty. Use a putty that closely matches the color of the wood.

CHAPTER SIX

DOORS

A well-made door can be more than a functional component, it can also add a good measure of visual appeal to your project. Two projects in this book have doors: the classic secretary desk and the traditional secretary desk. Both projects feature an upper cabinet with glazed frame-and-panel doors, while the lower cupboard has flush frame-and-panel doors.

The step-by-step instructions in this chapter explain how to make the glazed frame-and-panel doors for the secretary desks. As an option, you can build up the frames with moulding to hold the panels (either glass or wood) in place.

Various options for flush frame-and-panel doors are shown in chapter two, on page 52. Although this illustration shows the desktop inset, the same basic construction can be used to make a door.

Frame-and-panel door construction is similar in most applications. Sometimes the panel is wood; sometimes it's glass or wire grill or even tin plate. If you are a natural-born glazier, a leaded glass pattern could be used.

The size of the door components must match both the look and the structural requirements of the panel material. Single-strength glass is fairly heavy and, unlike wood, it does not expand or contract with changes in humidity. Glass panes should be cut undersize to "float" in the frame to allow for expansion and contraction of the wood components.

The various parts of frame-and-panel doors are shown below. Rabbets must be deep enough to capture the single-strength glass pane, which is about $1/8$" thick, glazer points and moulding. A wood panel can be thicker but requires less support at the back. That's because it can be flush with the back or inset and captured behind moulding.

Corner joints of the door frame should be strong to support the weight. Small doors can be made with mitered mortise and tenon, doweled or biscuit-joined corners. A through mortise and tenon is used for the secretary desk to maximize frame strength.

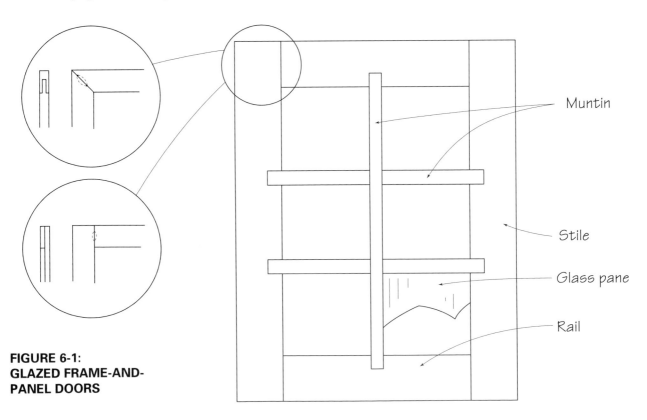

FIGURE 6-1:
GLAZED FRAME-AND-PANEL DOORS

Muntin

Stile

Glass pane

Rail

STEP 1

GLAZED FRAME-AND-PANEL DOORS

CONSTRUCTION STEPS

STEP 1

Cut the Rail Tenons

Begin the door construction by ripping stock for the rails and stiles.
Next, measure the door opening in
the upper cabinet, and cut the rail
and stile stock to length.

Once the stock is cut to width
and length, use the band saw (or
the table saw equipped with a dado
head) to cut the tenons on each
end of the rails.

STEP 2

Cut the Stile Mortises

The through mortises on the ends
of each stile are cut using the table
saw. As always, use a push stick
when working close to the blade
(safety guard removed for photo).
Through mortises can be cut on the
band saw as well. After the band
saw cut, you may have to flatten the
bottom of the mortise with a small
needle file.

STEP 2

STEP 3

Dry Fit Stiles and Rails

Lay out and mark the location of the
notches for the muntins, then use
the dado head to cut them out. Use
corner clamps to dry fit the stiles
and rails. Check all corners for fit
and squareness.

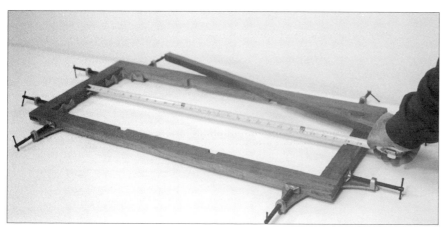

STEP 3

STEP 4

Mark the Dado Locations

Cut the muntins to length and width. The muntins should fit snugly in the notches, so make the cuts carefully.

After cutting the muntins to size, mark the location of the notches for the half lap joints.

STEP 4

STEP 5

Cut the Half Laps

Use the dado head to cut the notches in the muntins for the half lap joints. Set the dado depth to one-half the muntin thickness. Note the scrap board behind the stock to minimize tear-out at the back side of the dado cut.

STEP 5

STEP 6

Dry Assemble the Muntins

After cutting the half lap notches, dry assemble the parts and check that everything fits well.

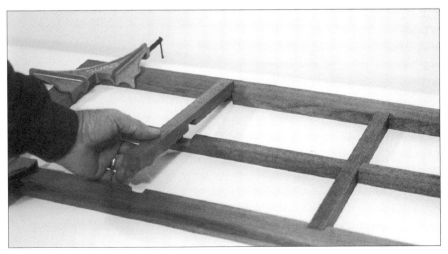

STEP 6

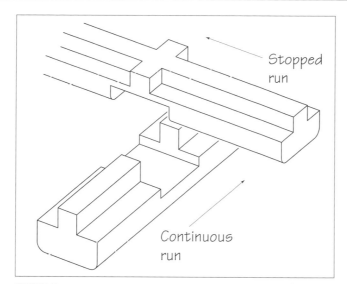

STEP 7

STEP 7

Plan the Rabbet Cuts

If you cut the muntin rabbets before the door parts are assembled (as I did), the rabbets on the single vertical muntin can be cut the full length; however, the rabbets on the two horizontal muntins must be stopped.

STEP 8

Cut the Rabbets

The table saw and dado head are used to cut the muntin rabbets. Use a pencil line to mark the stop locations on the horizontal muntins. A piece of tape on the saw table marks the leading edge of the dado cut. Feed the muntin until the pencil mark aligns with the tape, then turn off the saw and remove the stock. Repeat this procedure for each of the stopped cuts. Use a push stick and keep your hands well away from the dado head.

STEP 8

STEP 9

Cut the Rabbets (Drill Press Option)

The rabbets can also be cut with a router bit in the drill press. Before starting, set the drill press to its highest speed. Clamp a straightedge to the drill press table to limit the width of cut. The direction of feed should be such that the rotating cutter helps keep the workpiece against the straightedge.

STEP 9

STEP 10

Glue Door-Frame Assemblies

After a final dry fit, disassemble all parts and begin gluing the joints. Wipe a thin coat of glue on the mating surfaces and assemble. A thin scrap of wood makes a good spreader.

As a precaution, small dowels or pins (I used short brads, cut off to $^3/_{16}$") can be used where the muntins fit into the door stile. A pin will inhibit any lateral movement in the joint. This is probably unnecessary, but it doesn't hurt to add a little insurance.

STEP 11

Clamp the Doors

Make sure all the joints are seated, the sides are square and the assembled door is perfectly flat. Apply clamp pressure, and allow the glue to set.

STEP 12

Square the Corners

Whether you used the dado head or the router bit to cut the stopped rabbets, you'll find that both leave rounded corners. Use a sharp chisel to cut away the corners to a constant depth so the glass will fit flush in the frame.

STEP 10

STEP 11

STEP 12

STEP 13

STEP 14

STEP 15

STEP 13

Mould the Front Edges (Optional)

As an option, you can cut a moulded edge on the front of the frame. The drill press with a piloted router bit can be used here. Check the cut before starting, to make sure the pilot has enough stock to bear against. (Remember, most of the material on the back is removed by the earlier rabbet cut.) If the bit bears against fairly thin stock, use a bearing-guided pilot.

If your drill press table is small, add a plywood auxiliary table big enough to fully support the door. Depending on the hardness of the wood, the sharpness of the bit and the feed rate, you'll probably need to make successively deeper cuts until the desired depth and width are reached.

STEP 14

Router Option

If you prefer, the router can be used to cut the rabbets on the back and the moulding on the front. This operation is done after the doors have been glued. You'll need a piloted bit to do the job, preferably the bearing-guided type.

To make sure the router is fully supported throughout each cut, place a filler block (it must be the same thickness as the door-frame stock) in the panel opening.

STEP 15

Add Finish and Hinges

Final sand the doors, and apply the final finish. Once the finish is dry, mark the locations of the hinges and attach them to the door stiles.

Score the Glass

For about fifty dollars, you can have your local glass supplier cut a dozen glass panes; or for about ten dollars, you can buy a single sheet of glass and cut the panes yourself using a glass cutter.

The glass should be cut on a hard, flat surface, cushioned by some newspaper or old flooring material. Be sure to wear safety glasses and gloves. Check squareness of the glass. Working from the square sides, measure and mark the width of the panes. Clamp (or firmly hold) a straightedge along the marked line and run the glass cutter along the edge. Apply enough pressure so you hear a sound similar to that of paper tearing. If there is no sound, there is no score. It sometimes helps to tap along the score with the ball end of the glass cutter. Theoretically, this deepens the fracture at the score.

STEP 16

STEP 17

Snap the Glass

Place the scored line over a sharp edge, such as a length of straight-cut hardwood. Using moderate downward pressure, snap the glass at the score line.

Repeat the procedure to cut the panes to length.

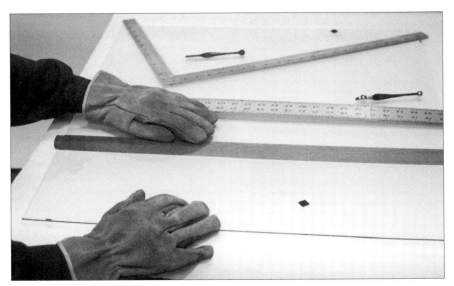

STEP 17

STEP 18

Install the Panes

Install the glass in frames using glazier points, or just rely on keeper moulding to hold the glass in place. You can purchase commercially made keeper moulding or use wood strips tacked in place.

STEP 18

CHAPTER SEVEN

DRAWERS

If you build a desk, it's likely you'll build drawers, maybe lots of drawers. Drawers provide a place for writing paper, pens and pencils, paper clips—and bills. Whatever drawer space you provide fills in due time. Like water, paper seeks its own level.

The three desks featured in chapter one each have a solitary center drawer set flush with the front aprons. The version with a frame-and-panel top and the lectern-desk version could include a bit more detail, such as veining around the drawer face, a raised panel or a lip on the facing.

Chapter two has three pedestal desks that contain either one, two or three drawers per tier and a shallow center drawer above the kneehole. The drawers can be varied to include deep file drawers, medium "shuck it in here" drawers and shallow drawers for shallow things. If you don't want the added width that's required to fit 11" or 14" files, the files can be placed perpendicular to the face.

Chapter two also presents the option of configuring the desk so it can be used with a computer. The craftsman-style pedestal desk has a slide-out keyboard tray in place of the kneehole drawer. In addition, the chapter includes thoughts on housing the computer's central processing unit (CPU) in one of the pedestals and, in place of the other pedestal, an open rack for your printer or plotter.

Weight is not of too much concern for most desk drawers. A ream of paper is fairly heavy, but when stored in a drawer of the same relative size, the surrounding dado grooves are close enough to the paper to support the weight.

DESIGNING DRAWERS

The weight and the depth of your desk or cabinet should be hefty enough to counterbalance a cantilevered drawer laden with heavy files or supplies. Long drawers, when fully extended, should not cause the desk to teeter on its front legs. Short drawers prevent this problem.

The three secretary desks in chapter three offer room for plenty of drawers. The classic secretary desk has just a single drawer between the writing surface and the lower cupboard. Of course, a number of variations are possible, such as eliminating the drawer entirely or adding a full chest of drawers in the base. The single drawer shown was constructed to include a center divider to help carry the weight of this wide span, but side-by-side drawers can also look good here.

All of the desks in this book can include an organizer. Within such an organizer, you might include small drawers to fit into one or more of the pigeonholes. These drawers might simply be trays that rest on horizontal members or full-fledged drawers with cases, runners and guides. For small drawers, I find the tray approach both easy and functional.

FLUSH-FRONT DRAWER (SEE CHAPTER ONE)

FLUSH-FRONT DRAWERS WITH CUT OUT (SEE CHAPTER TWO)

FLUSH-FRONT DRAWERS WITH PULLS (SEE CHAPTER THREE)

ANATOMY OF A DRAWER

In the step-by-step procedure that follows, all the drawer faces are $\frac{3}{4}$"-thick stock blind dovetailed into $\frac{3}{4}$"-thick sides. The back fits into dadoes cut in the sides. Two types of slides and guides are used on the projects in this book: (1) a wooden runner cut to fit in a groove in the drawer sides, and (2) commercial side-mounted roller slides.

Figure 7-1 (A and B) shows two ways to let in drawer bottoms to the face, back and sides of a drawer. Masonite, used for lightweight applications, can fit into a kerf cut inside the face, back and sides. Tempered Masonite ($\frac{1}{8}$"-thick) or doorskins work well for small drawer bottoms and larger, light-duty drawers. For heavier utility drawers that are used for storage or to support files, the bottom can be made from $\frac{1}{2}$" or $\frac{3}{4}$" edge-joined stock. The bottom can be beveled or coved to raise the dado well into the drawer face.

The drawer sides and back can be made of the same material as the furniture piece, or you can use such woods as alder, poplar or white oak. Medium density fiberboard (MDF) is used for drawer sides and back but generally not in fine furniture.

ATTACHING BACKS

Figure 7-1 (C, D and E) shows several ways that drawer backs can be attached to the sides. The dado set well in on the side (see figure 7-1C) holds at the back, while the bottom, inset around all the drawer box, keeps the glued back from loosening in the vertical direction. A box, or finger, joint can also be used (see figure 7-1D). However, for heavy-duty applications, this joint could pull out laterally over time unless it is dowel pinned down through the fingers. It's best to save this joint for small drawers. For an exceptionally strong joint, the backs can be through dovetailed (see figure 7-1E).

ANATOMY OF A DRAWER

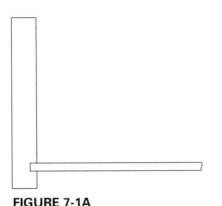

FIGURE 7-1A

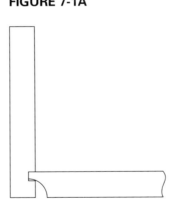

FIGURE 7-1B

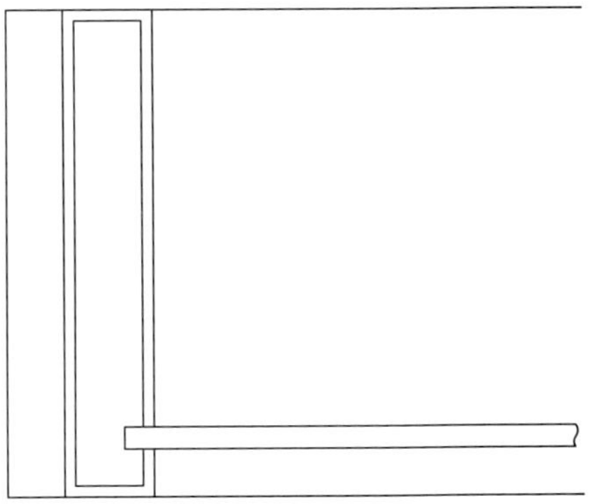

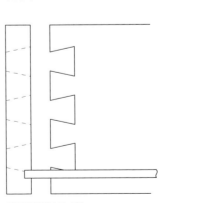

FIGURE 7-1C

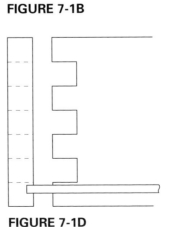

FIGURE 7-1D

FIGURE 7-1E

DOVETAILING THE DRAWER FACE TO THE SIDES

This classic drawer joint greatly increases the gluing surface of the joint and relies on the lateral strength of the wood to lock the face to the drawer sides. The maximum load on this joint occurs each time the drawer is pulled out. Butt joints at the face, even if let into a dado, can weaken over time. The inter-locking dovetails prevent this.

Hand-cut dovetails provide the maximum gluing surface, but those with a busy schedule often feel they have too many joints and too little time to cut them. This is where a dovetail template can come to the rescue.

Figure 7-1F shows a hand-cut dovetail and also a dovetail cut with a router jig. Note that the hand-cut dovetail results in a flat bottom, while the bottom of the router jig version is rounded. Lateral strength is para-mount, so the absence of gluing contact at the back is not crucial. For maximum joint strength, you could square the bottom of the dovetail with a chisel, as shown in figure 7-2.

Locating a row of dovetails, in both horizontal and vertical planes, is a function of the drawer width and length. Sometimes the drawer sides are inset to allow the face to cover a slide or a stop. In that case, the face is rabbeted on each end and the dovetail is cut into the rabbet.

Ideally, your dovetail joint layout begins with a full dovetail at the top. This doesn't always happen unless you plan the drawer height based on the dovetail pattern. If you wind up with less than half a dovetail at the end of the run, don't cut the corre-sponding dovetail in the face. Instead, cut the dovetail tab away and butt the lowest portion to the face. This eliminates vulnerable short tabs or tag ends.

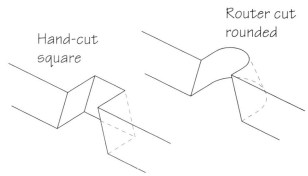

**FIGURE 7-1F:
ANATOMY OF A DOVETAIL**

**FIGURE 7-2:
SQUARE OFF THE DOVETAIL SLOT**

DOVETAILED DRAWER

CONSTRUCTION STEPS

STEP 1

Set Up the Dovetail Jig

Clamp the drawer face and a drawer side in the jig. The drawer face is clamped horizontally (facedown), far enough forward in the jig so the guide stops terminate the cuts just deep enough to encase the sides. The sides are clamped vertically, flush with the top of the horizontal face member, and offset by one dovetail finger.

Keep in mind that the alignment and depth placement in the jig are critical. The ends of the drawer sides are cut away forming dovetails; the pins are cut into the drawer face.

The first dovetail should begin comfortably below the drawer top. If possible, center the bank of dovetails along the stock width, leaving adequate material at the ends. Don't rout if the positioning produces less than half a dovetail where it runs out the bottom. Instead, finish the joint by hand.

STEP 1

STEP 2

STEP 3

STEP 4

Cut the Dovetails

Unless your dovetailing bit has a shank that is the same diameter as the guide, you'll need to attach a router guide bushing (in this example, ³/₈" diameter) to the router base. Set the bit depth to one-half the thickness of the drawer face.

Pass the router across the vertical end to form evenly spaced dovetails. Rout the receiving dovetail slots in the end of the horizontal face for a distance equal to the side thickness. Keep both sets of cuts at the same depth setting.

STEP 3

Dry Fit the Drawers

Dry fit the drawer assembly. Rasp, file or sand the dovetail sides and slots for a snug press fit.

STEP 4

Cut the Grooves

If you haven't already done so, dado the groove for the drawer bottom in the face, back and sides. If you are using wooden slides in the guides, cut the groove in each side at this time as well.

If your drawer face has a cutout handle (such as the craftsman-style pedestal desk), it's best to band saw the cutout before the drawer parts are assembled.

Glue Up the Drawer

Add a thin coat of glue to the mating dovetail joint surfaces, then assemble the parts.

STEP 5

Clamp

Add clamps and apply firm pressure to the joints. Check for squareness before setting aside to dry.

STEP 6

SMALL FINGER-JOINT DRAWER

Finger joints can be used in small drawers such as might be found in the desk organizers featured in chapter one. The strength of this joint makes it a good candidate for attaching backs to larger drawers as well. The fingers can be as thin as a saw blade kerf or made to any thickness you think fits the design.

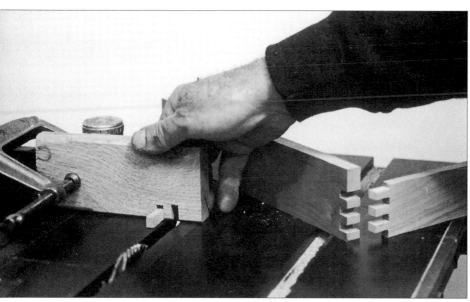

STEP 1

CONSTRUCTION STEPS

STEP 1
Make the Jig

You can purchase commercially made finger-joint jigs, but for a fraction of the cost, you can make your own. Commercial jigs usually have limited options for joint spacing, but making the jig yourself allows you to establish any joint spacing.

The jig is simply a short, narrow, notched board that is clamped to your table saw miter gauge. Use a piece of straight and true scrap stock for the board. It is best to use a hardwood here so the jig board holds up throughout the process.

Set the dado blade to make a cut that equals the finger thickness you've chosen. Then raise the dado blade to a height equal to the thickest of the parts to be joined. For example, if you are joining a ³/₄"-thick drawer face to ¹/₂"-thick sides, you would raise the dado blade to a ³/₄" height.

Make the first dado cut through the jig board. Next, offset this cut a distance equal to the width of the first cut, and make a second dado cut at this location. Clamp the jig board to the miter guide at the second cut location.

The projecting tab can now be made. Cut it to equal the thickness of the finger and the height of the thinnest members to be joined. Once cut, insert the tab in the first slot so it protrudes from the jig board by about ¹/₂".

Cut the Finger Joints

The first cut on the drawer face should be one tab thickness from the top, so butt the top surface against the protruding tab and cut the first slot. Then place this slot over the tab and cut the next finger (see photo at right). Continue this process until you run out of wood.

If all the drawer parts are the same thickness, there is no need to change the dado-head height. If the thicknesses differ, adjust the blade height to match the thickness of the member being let in.

Since the drawer face starts with a tab, the drawer sides start with a cut. Align what would be the top of the side to the far side of the second cut you made in the auxiliary face. For the second cut, butt the first cut against the tab to space the first finger. Third and subsequent fingers are spaced by placing the last slot over the tab.

It is wise to test these distances on some scrap pieces before dadoing all the parts. You don't want to find out after the job is done that the finger widths could have been a bit narrower for an easier fit.

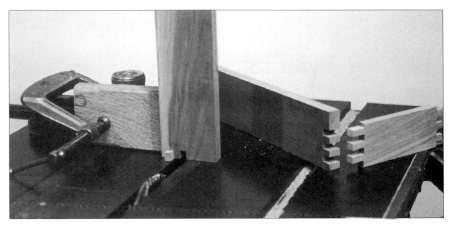

STEP 2

STEP 3

STEP 3

Add the Bottom

Check to make sure the drawer front, back and sides fit nicely. If all looks OK, cut a groove in each part to receive the bottom. Next, add glue to the mating surfaces of the finger joints, and assemble all the parts. Make sure the drawer is square. After the glue has set, sand the faces and tabs flush. Finish with fine sandpaper.

DRAWER-MAKING NOTES

SETTING THE JIG FOR ODD DRAWERS

The pedestal desks in chapter two have faces that are ³/₄"-thick, while the sides are ¹/₂"-thick. Also, some of the drawers have faces that are wider than the sides. That means the dovetails begin at the side height, as if this were the top of the drawer facing. The same positions in the dovetailing template are used, except the dovetail grooves are shorter to match the thinner sides.

ROUNDING THE EDGES

The edges of the drawer faces and sides can be rounded with a router or shaper before assembly. As shown, the drill press can also serve as a router. Use a piloted router bit, and set the drill press to its highest speed.

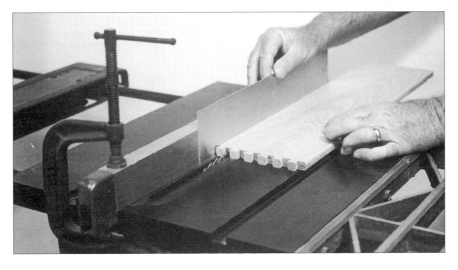

KERF-WIDENING TIP

To create a slightly wider groove for the drawer bottom (without having to readjust the rip fence), make a second cut with a thin strip of metal between the work and the rip fence. The groove is widened by an amount equal to the metal thickness.

CENTER DIVIDER OPTION

A wide drawer can be reinforced by dadoing a center divider into the front and back. Grooves cut into both sides of the divider support the Masonite at the drawer center.

INSET DOVETAILS

Inset dovetails are often used in conjunction with commercial drawer slides. The drawer front overlaps the sides to hide the slides from view when the drawer is closed.

JIG SETUP FOR INSET DOVETAILS

Most dovetail jigs can be used to cut inset dovetails. The drawer face is first rabbeted on each end before it is secured in the jig. The dovetail pins are cut into the edges of the rabbet.

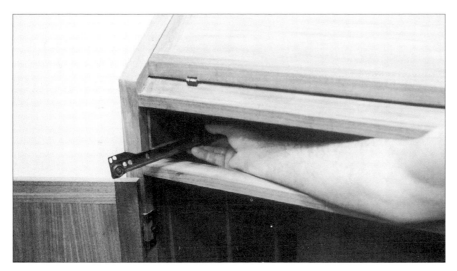

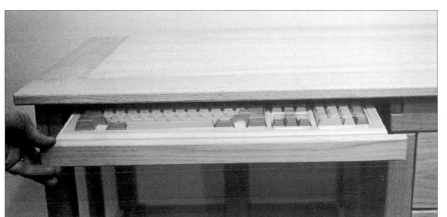

RUNNERS AND GUIDES

Whether you build guides and slides or buy them, they should allow for smooth and positive operation of the drawers. Most commercial drawer slides (see illustration at left) work well and can be installed with a minimum of fuss. Commercial slides require specific spacing between the drawer opening and the drawer sides, so it's a good idea to have the slides on hand before making the drawers. Woodworking mail-order companies offer a wide variety of slides (see Sources of Supply on page 126).

Runners that support the drawers can be fitted into a groove cut in the drawer sides, or the drawers can slide on a shelf (or even cleats). "Achieve clearance without slop" is the thought for the day when cutting and fitting drawers.

KEYBOARD SLIDES

The keyboard slide attaches to the underside of the top. It offers some up-and-down adjustment to allow for various keyboard thicknesses. This is the same slide used in the craftsman-style pedestal desk shown in chapter two.

KEYBOARD TRAY

The keyboard tray is made from plywood. The facing is one-half the width of the desk rails, allowing your hands to comfortably reach the keyboard.

CHAPTER EIGHT

ORGANIZERS

DESIGN AND CONSTRUCTION

A well-designed organizer can improve both the appearance and the utility of your desk. The pigeonholes, nooks, dividers and drawers provide an assortment of places that can help keep your desktop organized. Indeed, an organizer is the perfect answer for desk clutter.

When designing an organizer, it is important to maintain the established "look" of the desk. The step-by-step procedure in this chapter explains how to make the organizer for the writing desk with solid top featured in chapter one. This desk, with its open-plan view, requires a low-profile organizer. The square tapered legs with abrupt angles call for a certain squareness to the organizer. The slanted angles used in the sides and dividers follow the taper lines. The organizer matrix retains the sharp edges used for the desk. If your

design includes turned tapered legs, a half-round edge treatment can complement the overall design. Likewise, the ends of the organizer can be either concave or convex arcs. Think in terms of "what goes, and what doesn't?"

OK, so I gave in and bought a biscuit-cutter attachment for my router. This is my first affair, so please be kind. Biscuit joints are far easier to dry fit than doweled joints, which was my justification for purchasing this tool, and this acquisition is going to save me time and effort when I build future projects.

The top of the organizer butts to the sides, but it can also be placed on top of the sides, either flush or overhanging on each end. The top can also be located a bit lower so the top edge of the sides extends above the shelf by ¼" to ½".

CONSTRUCTION STEPS

STEP 1
Biscuit-Slot the Top

Cut the organizer top to length and width. Set the biscuit-cutter depth to about half the thickness of the wood being joined. When cutting into the thickness, you have the full support of the flat face for the router base during the cut and plenty of run to extend the guidelines so they can be seen beyond the base of the router or the jig pictured here.

The center lines that mark the biscuit locations should be extended well beyond the diameter of the router attachment base. Begin your cut at the left limit mark, press the cutter into the end and feed right to the opposite end.

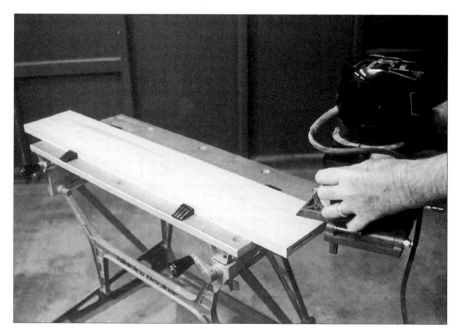

STEP 1

STEP 2

Biscuit-Slot the Sides

Cut the organizer sides to length and width, then lay out and mark the angled front edge on each one. Use a band saw to make the angled cuts. Smooth the sawn edges with a hand plane or sandpaper.

Don't change the cutter depth setting on your biscuit cutter. The beauty of this method is that you maintain the same distance from adjoining surfaces so the pieces assemble flush. Although the router guide is cumbersome, it is handy in maintaining slots that match in depth and length.

The guideline marks for these cuts extend across the ¾" thickness; therefore, they are hidden by the cutter base. Place an auxiliary block behind the stock, and flush to the top edge. Extend these biscuit center lines beyond the cutter table to guide your cut.

I used the edge of the auxiliary block as my guide. This provided a flat working surface for the router base. Reposition the block to the next center line and repeat. Unlike doweling, you have some horizontal forgiveness in these joints; they don't have to be right on in the horizontal plane.

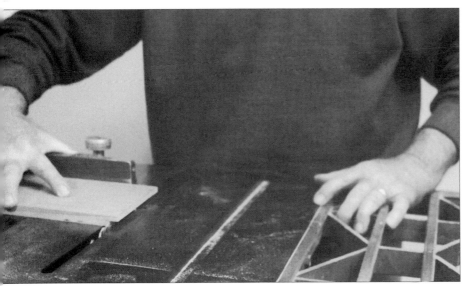

STEP 3

Cut the Bottom Rabbets

Using the table saw and dado head, cut the rabbets on each end of the organizer bottom. The miter gauge supports the stock as it is passed over the cutter.

Dado the Back, Top and Bottom

Cut the back to size, then lay out and mark the locations of the various dadoes on the back, top and bottom. Note that the dadoes are stopped short of the front edge on the top. On the bottom, the dadoes are cut from the front to back edges. Next, replace the miter gauge with the rip fence, and cut the groove (for the back) in both the top and bottom.

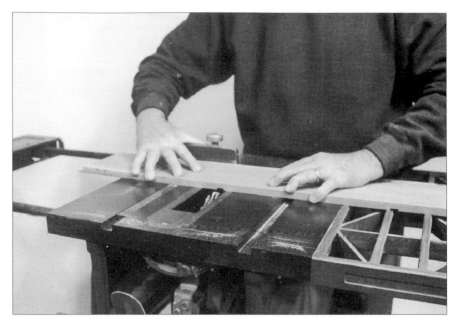

STEP 4

Dado the Sides

The stopped dado (to accept the back of the organizer) can be cut with the dado-head cutter, rip fence and miter gauge. The rip fence serves to locate the dado at the correct distance from the end of the stock. The miter gauge supports the stock during the cut. A stopblock, clamped to the saw table, establishes the length of the dado.

To cut the dado on the other side piece, move the miter gauge to the opposite side of the saw table. Reset the stopblock, and again use the miter gauge to make the cut. Most rip fences can't be moved to the opposite side of the saw, so for this cut, use marked lines to establish the dado location.

Each side also has a pair of stopped grooves, one for the bottom rabbet and one for the shelf. The dado head can again be used here.

A router, straight bit and edge guide can also cut the dadoes and grooves in the side piece. Also, a router table, if you have one, would be especially useful here.

STEP 5

STEP 6

STEP 6

Square the Corners

The dado head leaves rounded corners where the cut is stopped. So, too, does a router bit, if you used that method. Finish the stopped grooves by squaring the corners with a sharp chisel.

STEP 7

STEP 7

Dry Fit the Parts

Final sand all the organizer parts through 220-grit. Once sanded, dry assemble the parts to make sure all fit well.

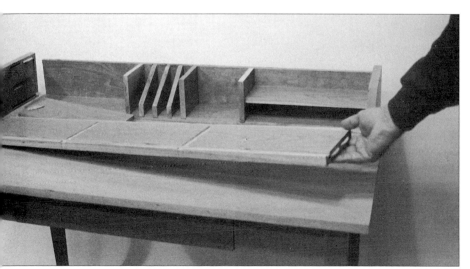

STEP 8

STEP 8

Assemble

Apply glue to the mating surfaces, and assemble the parts. Clamp firmly, and allow to dry overnight.

AUXILIARY DRAWERS

Just about any pigeonhole is a candidate for a small drawer. Two drawers at opposing ends can add symmetry, balance and interest to your desk. Chapter seven discusses the construction of small finger-joint drawers.

OTHER VARIATIONS

Organizers can be made in any number of shapes and configurations. A few of them are shown in figure 8-9.

The design options range from a simple backstop (not shown) that prevents pencils and paper from slipping out the back, to a low-profile organizer, to an enclosed organizer, to an enclosure covered with a hinged lid or tamboured rolltop. These options apply as well to the pedestal desk projects shown in chapter two.

Tambours lend themselves both to traditional rolltop desks and contemporary designs. Any large organizer enclosure is a candidate for a tamboured cover. If you want to add a tambour cover to the organizer, rout a tambour track in the shell sides, providing enough track for the tambour to retract the desired amount.

Tambours can be purchased ready-made, or you can make your own by cementing the individual tambour strips to canvas. When routing the tambour track, make sure all radii are large enough to allow the tambours and the canvas backing to make the bend. Also

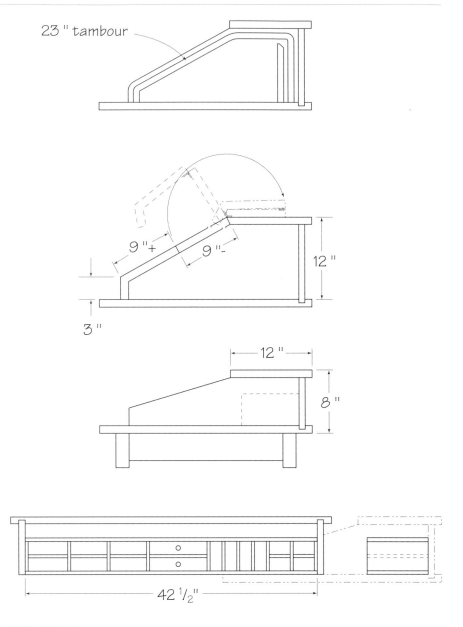

FIGURE 8-9:
ORGANIZER OPTIONS

make sure the tambour thickness is such that it can slide through the radii without binding.

Also shown in figure 8-9 is a lift-top work surface, which can be either folded back or hinged. It adds an interesting feature to the organizer.

ATTACHMENT

Section A-A in figure 8-9A shows two options for attaching the organizer to the desktop. Locating the organizer sides just outside the desk aprons allows you to drive screws through the underside of the desktop and into the bottom edge of the sides. Also, as shown, you can dowel the organizer sides to the desktop.

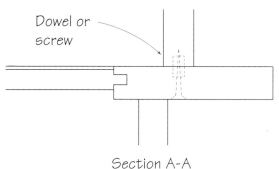

Dowel or screw

Section A-A

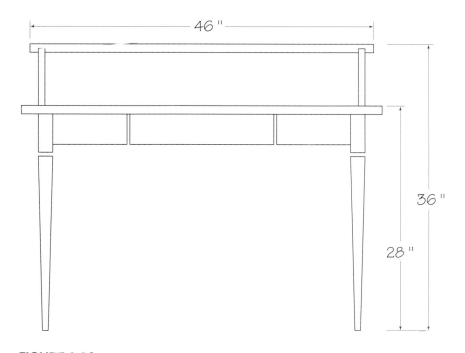

46"

36"

28"

**FIGURE 8-9A:
ORGANIZER OPTIONS**

CHAPTER NINE

FINISHING

As a general rule, the finish you like to apply to small wooden projects can also be used on larger furniture. The oil finishes, however, are exceptions to the rule. An oil finish may be fine for a serving tray or a small box, but it requires too much ongoing maintenance when applied to a dining table, pedestal desk or secretary desk. To provide better protection against coffee stains, alcohol spills and the inevitable condensation that forms on cold glasses in the summertime, you need an overcoat of varnish, lacquer or one of the "poly-" products.

What you put between the wood and the overcoat is your choice, dictated somewhat by the look you want and the surface characteristics of the wood. An acquaintance once remarked, "You don't want to candy the finish too much," which means don't cover over the natural figuring, except to blend coloring or match adjacent furniture.

Light-colored woods tend to darken as they weather, and dark woods generally bleach lighter under the sun's heat and ultraviolet rays. This effect is good as it mellows the piece over time.

A matte or satin finish has a pleasing, soft look. This can be achieved by using Deft or any of the "-thane" products. Some of the earlier polyurethane finishes tended to yellow, but modern products are formulated for a clearer, nonyellowing finish. Use a gloss Varathane, spar varnish or lacquer for the Oriental, high-gloss finishes.

There are three grades or types of varnish: short, medium and long.

The grade is based on the amount of oil used per 100 pounds of resin. More resin produces a harder, faster drying varnish; more oil produces a softer, more elastic, slower drying varnish.

Many wood finishers swear by the disposable foam brushes. In my opinion, they don't produce the same results as a quality natural boar bristle brush. Save the nylon bristle for latex. Natural bristle is best because it has natural splits at the ends. Some synthetic brushes try to duplicate this splitting but without much success.

Enough rambling. I finished the cherry writing desk (see chapter one) and the walnut secretary desk (see chapter three) with three coats of Clearthane finish. I didn't stain or color the wood before applying the finish. I gave each coat a light sanding using 320-grit or 400-grit paper, using a tack rag to remove the sanding dust. The oak pedestal desk (see chapter three) was to have a wipe-on/wipe-off stain, followed by the same Clearthane finish, but the family "committee" opted for an unstained finish.

SANDING

When finishing wood, the first order of business is to create a flat, smooth surface that is free of tool marks. Usually a 100- or 120-grit sandpaper can get the wood surface to this point. If you need to round or slightly soften sharp edges, start with a coarser grit, then follow with 120-grit.

Use 220-grit sandpaper to ready the surface for stain or overcoat. The paper can be used in a palm sander or sanding block or as a three-fold sheet for hand-sanding. The three folds work well; one-third of the sheet is doing the work, the third folded inside keeps the paper from sliding on itself, and the top third against your hand increases the grip. Unfolded sandpaper gives you little to grasp, and a single-fold piece tends to slide on the smooth inside surfaces while sanding.

MASKING ADJACENT SURFACES

Remember, plywood has a veneer layer that is mighty thin. When using a power sander to finish a solid-wood edging applied to the plywood, use a piece of cardboard or heavy paper to protect the plywood as the edging is sanded. Once the plywood and edging are flush, they can both be sanded at the same time with fine-grit sandpapers.

The use of masking or edging tape is not recommended on raw wood. No matter how tack free and friendly the adhesive is, some wood fibers are going to be pulled from the wood as the tape is removed. Tape is less likely to be a problem over sealed wood. Removing the tape by pulling it 90° from the lay of the tape is kinder to the surface below.

TACK CLOTH

Before applying a finish, make sure the surfaces are well brushed, wiped or vacuumed in order to pick up any remaining sanding dust. Wipe the entire surface with a tack cloth, which is simply a piece of cheesecloth wet with a little varnish and turpentine to make the cloth sticky. As you wipe the project with the tack cloth, the surface dust sticks to the varnish. You can make your own tack rag or buy one at most any hardware store.

It's a good idea to clean up the shop a little as well. It doesn't have to be "clean room" clean, but the potential for airborne dust particles should be minimized.

STAINING

If you want to darken the wood or lighten it using a whitewash, most any home-improvement center or paint store is likely to have what you need. Unfinished-furniture stores also offer a good selection of wood stains and finishes that might be just right for your project.

Before staining your project, always test the material first to make sure you are going to like the result. For wipe-on stains, use a soft cotton cloth and carefully follow all the directions on the product label.

CLEAR FINISHES

Some clear finishes contain a reactive solvent, like lacquer thinner, that can streak or mottle the stain. Work an area only once and go on.

Don't linger, and don't go back or you'll pick up the undercoat. Keep a wet edge. Don't work too far away from the wet area. All semigloss, matte or satin finish products need to be stirred thoroughly and often to keep the dulling agent suspended in solution.

Apply two or three coats of the top sealer, sanding lightly between applications (read and follow the manufacturer's instructions). The final coat could be hand rubbed with a little carnauba wax or furniture polish.

PREFINISH PARTS

In chapter three, before glazing the paneled doors of the secretary desk, the glass frames were prefinished. It's easier to prefinish than to try and finish the frames with the glass in place. Likewise, you can clean the glass before it is installed. Then when assembled, the doors are ready to hang. This approach also applies to shelves and other components that can be difficult to finish in place.

FINISH INSIDE AND OUT

To prevent warp, seal the inside as well as outside surfaces of your desk project. Your piece stands a better chance of becoming an heirloom by going this extra yard.

CLEANUP

Clean the brushes in a series of coffee cans (or you can buy empty paint cans to use for this purpose). Wipe the excess from the brush, then clean it in the first bath. I use a second bath of mineral spirits, followed by a third dunking in lacquer thinner. If you cover the cans and let them stand for a time, the residue settles to the bottom. The next time you use the bath, pour the clear solvent off the top, then shake or otherwise wipe the bottom clean and reuse the solvent. This way you dispose of only the sediment.

For some woodworkers, the care and feeding of brushes involves storing brushes wet by suspending them in linseed oil. In my opinion, this procedure gums up the works. Instead, remove the excess solvent by gently shaking the brush. When the brush is almost dry, use a brush comb to smooth the bristles, then hang the brush on a hook.

Don't dump the solvent down the kitchen sink or in the backyard. Carelessly dumped solvents will contaminate the earth's water, either as runoff to the rivers and oceans or by percolating into the ground water. If your finishing projects are infrequent and you must dispose of used solvent, save it until a household waste disposal day is scheduled near your home.

CUSTOM DESIGN

As a woodworker, you have the distinct ability to design and build custom furniture that can complement its environs. Scale, proportion, craftsmanship and finish are fundamental design considerations. These factors represent the aesthetic qualities—the style—of your piece. If that same piece of custom furniture serves as a functional work area for the family, whether used while standing, sitting or reclining, you must also consider functional qualities, including clearance, reach and mechanics. Both sets of design parameters must be considered and accomplished together in order to achieve your overall design objective.

Proportion is important, but simply being proportionally pleasing is not enough. A piece of furniture must also serve its intended function, fitting both the space and the task. A study of ergonomics can guide your design selection.

The primary objectives of industrial workplace designers are efficiency, productivity, reduced fatigue and operator safety. Such objectives are important to the user of a writing desk as well. Optimum seating height, adequate leg room, comfortable work height and achievable reach standards apply as much in your home as they do in industry.

Certain norms and design parameters have been developed to fit the typical or average person. The big advantage of designing and building your own furniture is that "typical" is replaced by "specific." You can design and build for a target population—your family.

The height of a writing surface is generally 27" to 29", while the accompanying chair has a standard

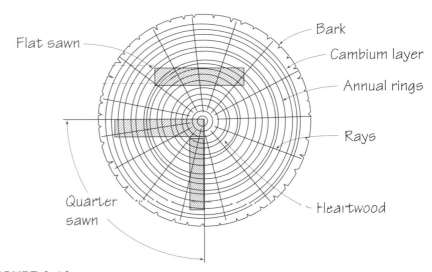

FIGURE A-1A: MILLCUTS

height of about 17". If a favorite desk chair is above or below the ergonomically correct height, you can adjust the desk height to fit the chair. The critical dimension here is clearance between a persons's lap and the underside of the desk (or desk drawer). If necessary, deviate from the norm to fit the function with the user, while preserving the aesthetic proportions and the overall "look" of the piece.

Height also plays into the design. The first two writing desks featured in chapter one are presented at table height, but they could be somewhat higher. The lectern desk, also in chapter one, is an example of a tall desk.

YOUR STYLE

Charles Eames designed chairs for comfort and style. Sam Maloof's designs are no less comfortable but exhibit his distinctive signature. Lesser-known craftspeople have a distinctive style as well, and while not commercially or artistically known, they still impart unique flair and personality. Don't be afraid to add your special style and personality to the desk you build.

CHARACTERISTICS OF WOOD

Seasonal changes in humidity can affect wood. During the winter, the air is generally dry (especially in heated homes), so a board tends to lose moisture, causing it to shrink in width. In the summer, when the air is humid, a board absorbs moisture, causing it to grow in width. (Moisture has little effect on the length of a board.) Plywood is not affected by changes in moisture content because of its cross-grained construction.

The grain pattern of a board is related to how it is cut from a log (see figure A-1A). When viewed from the end of the stock, flat-sawn boards have tangential rings (see figure A-1B). Flat-sawn boards are also called slash grain, flat grain or plain-sawn. Quartersawn boards have radial rings (see figure A-1C). Boards that are quartersawn are sometimes called vertical grain, straight grain, comb grain and edge grain. Quartersawn boards are less likely to cup, and they also expand and contract less with changes in moisture content.

You can purchase boards that are

planed smooth on two sides (S2S), two sides and one edge (S3S) or two sides and two edges (S4S). Having at least one planed edge provides you with a straight, true edge to work from on the table saw.

Thickness-planed stock is generally most convenient to use. Boards that are thickness planed are easier to inspect for appearance and figure. The result is less spoilage. Assuming you go this route, also inspect the boards for such defects as cup, bow and twist (also called wind—rhymes with find). Boards with any of these defects (see figure A-2) should remain in the lumber rack. Boards that are straight and true are hassle free, or almost so.

Boards purchased rough sawn must be surfaced on a thickness planer. If you don't own a thickness planer, check with your local lumberyard or millwork shop as most of them will surface lumber for a nominal fee.

PERIOD FURNITURE

All that we see and all that we have has evolved from the past. From the early Spartan furnishing represented by Shaker furniture to the ornate Louis XV offerings, what we build takes a little from both ends of the spectrum and adds something from in between, too.

Writing desks are all used for the same task—writing. The designs vary according to the chosen base, enclosure and appointments. Indeed, there is similarity among the writing desks in this book. The writing desk with solid top (in chapter one), when enclosed, begins to take on the characteristics of the secretary desk (in chapter three); and a short secretary desk with a drop front isn't too far afield from the pedestal desks (in chapter two).

Generally, secretary desks represent a more elegant period. They are

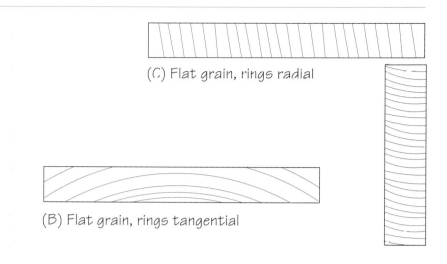

(C) Flat grain, rings radial

(B) Flat grain, rings tangential

FIGURE A-1B, A-1C: MILLCUTS

a refined piece, with or without a glass-enclosed upper bookshelf. However, as shown in the country-style version, the same carcase can be built from lesser-grade lumber and left open with simple cupboard doors in the base.

There are three basic desk designs in the book: the writing desk with solid top, the craftsman-style pedestal desk and the classic-style secretary desk. All three are built using different methods.

The writing desk with solid top is made from solid wood. Edge-joined boards make up the top. The prima-

ry structural component is the top, to which all else is attached.

The pedestal desk projects are frame-and-panel construction. A matrix of rails and stiles are filled with panels. The rails span corner posts to form a box.

The secretary desk is built using premium plywood veneer capped and edged in matching solid woods. Structural stability comes from basic box construction.

The materials and methods were selected for illustrative purposes. Any one of the methods is suitable for any project.

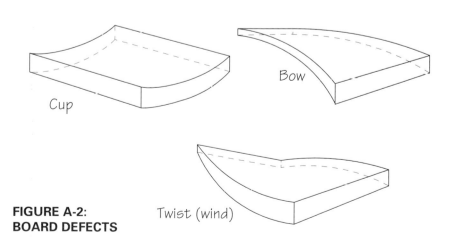

Cup

Bow

Twist (wind)

FIGURE A-2: BOARD DEFECTS

SOURCES OF SUPPLY

ADAMS WOOD PRODUCTS
974 Forest Drive
Morristown, TN 37814
(615) 587-2942
turned table legs, cabriole legs

CONSTANTINE'S
2050 Eastchester Road
Bronx, NY 10461
(800) 223-8087
general woodworking supplies

GARRETT WADE
161 Avenue of the Americas
New York, NY 10013-1299
(800) 221-2942
general woodworking supplies

OSBORN WOOD PRODUCTS
Route 3, Box 551
Toccoa, GA 30577
(800) 849-8876
turned table legs, cabriole legs

TRENDLINE'S
375 Beacham Street
Chelsea, MA 02150
(800) 767-9999
general woodworking supplies

WOODCRAFT
210 Wood County Industrial Park
P.O. Box 1686
Parkersburg, WV 26102-1686
(800) 225-1153
general woodworking supplies

THE WOODWORKER'S STORE
21801 Industrial Boulevard
Rogers, MN 55374-9514
(800) 279-4441
general woodworking supplies

WOODWORKER'S SUPPLY
1108 North Glenn Road
Casper, WY 82601
(800) 645-9292
general woodworking supplies

INDEX